I0101917

NOBLE COW

MUNCHING GRASS

LOOKING CURIOUS

AND

JUST HANGING AROUND

By
Dr. Sahadeva dasa

B.com., FCA., AICWA., PhD
Chartered Accountant

SOUL
SCIENCE UNIVERSITY

Soul Science University Press
www.cowism.com

Readers interested in the subject matter of this
book are invited to correspond with the publisher at:
SoulScienceUniversity@gmail.com   +91 98490 95990

First Edition: January 2012

Soul Science University Press expresses its gratitude to the
Bhaktivedanta Book Trust International (BBT), for the use of quotes by His
Divine Grace A.C.Bhaktivedanta Swami Prabhupada.
Copyright Bhaktivedanta Book Trust International (BBT)
Also we thank CareForCows.org for some of their pictures.

ISBN 978-81-909760-8-4

Published by:
Dr. Sahadeva dasa for Soul Science University Press

Website by :
E. Karnika Yashwant (Ens.org.in)

Printed by:
Rainbow Print Pack, Hyderabad

To order a copy write to chandra@rgbooks.co.in
or buy online: at www.rgbooks.co.in

"So from the cows, the milk. And from the milk we can make hundreds of vitaminous foodstuff, hundreds. They're all palatable. So such a nice animal, faithful, peaceful, and beneficial. After taking milk from it, if we kill, does it look very well? Even after the death, the cows supply the skin for your shoes. It is so beneficial. You see. Even after death. While living, he gives you nice milk. You cannot reject milk from the human society. As soon as there is a child born, milk immediately required. Old man, milk is life. Diseased person, milk is life. Invalid, milk is life. So therefore Krishna is teaching by His practical demonstration how He loves this innocent animal, cow."

-Srila Prabhupada

<u>By The Same Author</u>
Oil-Final Countdown To A Global Crisis And Its Solutions
End of Modern Civilization And Alternative Future
To Kill Cow Means To End Human Civilization
Cow And Humanity - Made For Each Other
Cows Are Cool - Love 'Em!
Wondrous Glories of Vraja
Modern Foods - Stealing Years From Your Life
Lets Be Friends! - A Curious, Calm Cow
(More information on availability at the back)

Contents

The Author

Preface

The holocaust didn't end, it's rampant, it's merely turned to other species.

What is your definition of holocaust? Is it a massacre of human beings, or a massacre of innocent beings? All over the globe, we murder 55 billion land animals and 90 billion marine animals every year. Not for health, survival, sustenance, or self-defense - people eat meat, fish and eggs for 4 reasons: habit, tradition, convenience, and taste.

Jewish author Isaac Bashevis Singer, who received the Nobel Prize in Literature in 1978, made the comparison in several of his stories, including Enemies, A Love Story, The Penitent, and The Letter Writer. In the latter the protagonist says, "In relation to [animals], all people are Nazis; for the animals, it is an eternal Treblinka." In The Penitent the protagonist says "when it comes to animals, every man is a Nazi."

Belgian writer Marguerite Yourcenar also made the comparison. She wrote that if we haven't accepted the inhumane transportation of animals to the slaughterhouses we wouldn't have accepted the transportation of human being to the concentration camps. In another article, making the same connection, she wrote that every act of cruelty suffered by thousands of living creatures is a crime against humanity.

J. M. Coetzee, who received the Nobel Prize in Literature in 2003, invoked the image of the slaughterhouse in describing the Nazi's treatment of Jews: "... in the 20th century, a group of powerful and bloody-minded men in Germany hit on the idea of adapting the methods of the industrial stockyard, as pioneered and perfected in Chicago, to the slaughter — or what they preferred to call the processing — of human beings."

Contrary to political and religious dogma, animals do not belong to us. They are not commodities. They're not property and they're not inanimate stupid objects that can't think and feel. That Cartesian way of looking at animals like they're machines is outdated and quite frankly, 100% insane.

In 2001, Meat.org included an "Animal Holocaust" section containing photographs of animals with captions such as "Holocaust Victim," arguing that it's "easy to see the resemblance of the systematic destruction and slaughter of over six million Jews by the Nazis before and during World War II and the over 20 million animals that are executed every day in America alone. Many of the Jews of the Holocaust were transported to concentration camps in cattle cars to their death. The concentration camps very much resemble the common slaughterhouses of today."

In his autobiography, My Life and Work (1922), Ford revealed that his inspiration for assembly-line production came from a visit he made as a young man to a Chicago slaughterhouse. "I believe that this was the first moving line ever installed. The idea [of the assembly line] came in a general way from the overhead trolley that the Chicago packers use in dressing beef." A Swift and Company publication from that time described the division-of-labor principle that so impressed Ford: "The slaughtered animals, suspended head downward from a moving chain, or conveyor, pass from workman to workman, each of whom performs some particular step in the process." It was but one step from the industrialized slaughter of animals to the assembly-line mass murder of people.

Why is it always such a surprise to us humans that other animals have feelings, form bonds, and relationships and have ways of communicating still not understood by us. Are we really so stupid that we believe we are the only species that do this?

The great blind spot of our modern Civilization for that matter is the mistreatment and disregard for non-human animals in nearly every capacity.

How would you feel if the day you were born somebody else had already planned the day of your execution? That's what it's like to be a cow, pig, chicken or turkey on this planet. This type of behavior is inexcusable and unbecoming of a species that claims to understand right from wrong. The animals have not done one single thing to us to deserve the wrath and cruelty that we hurl on them.

This book deals with the ability of animals to feel, perceive or be conscious, or to have subjective experiences. Eighteenth century philosophers used the concept to distinguish the ability to think ("reason") from the ability to feel ("sentience"). In modern western philosophy, sentience is the ability to have sensations or experiences. For Eastern philosophy, sentience is a metaphysical quality of all things that requires respect and care. The concept is central to the philosophy of animal rights, because sentience is necessary for the ability to suffer, which entails certain rights.

Sahadeva dasa

1st January 2012
Secunderabad, India

Cow Separated From Owner

Goes On Hunger Strike

This is a true story from Taiwan. Chen Chuan-li, 75, has been raising cows since he was only eight years old. He knows the moods and habits of the animals well, can recite every phrase and proverb in Chinese having to do with them, and is the head-to-tail authority on everything bovine.

In recent years, however, declining health forced Chen to part with almost all his cattle. One cow, however, was especially dear to his heart and he refused to let her go.

When Chen suffered a stroke last year, he followed doctor's orders religiously and went to the hospital regularly for rehabilitation exercises, all so that he could return to his beloved cow Ah Mei and tend to her.

In spite of his efforts, however, Chen could not been regain enough of his former health to drive an ox cart safely. His family was concerned that he could fall down from the cart and injure himself.

Thus just before

the Lunar New Year, Chen made the painful decision to sell his cart and his cow for NT$150,000 (US$5,128).

Chan says that if he were still in good health, he would not have sold the pair even for NT$200,000. He turned down an exchange offer of a Mercedes-Benz made by an elderly Japanese man two years ago.

Ah Mei did not adjust well to her new family afterwards, however. For the first three days after she was sold, she would not eat at all, refusing to drink even water.

In desperation, the new owner called on Chen to come over and reason with her. "Okay, you and I are splits now," Chen told her. "You have a new owner, be a good cow now and eat your food!" Only then did Ah Mei begin to eat again.

The new owner, surnamed Chien, understands the depth of Chen's love for the cow. Chen would even blame him for using the wrong kind of grass for the cow, according to Chien.

"He would say, with tears in his eyes, 'That grass isn't good enough for her!'" Chien recalls.

Seeing the depth of the affection between the two, Chien promised to treat the cow well.

(Reported in the Liberty Times, Feb. 13th 2011)

Unlike Ah Mei, cows in modern times are no longer considered to be sentient beings. They have been reduced to the status of mere meat bags, to be enjoyed as dinner or to be worn as suede suits.

> *"There's nothing like sitting back and talking to your cows."*
> —Russell Crowe

2.

A Motherless Child

Finds A Mother

This is story of Tha Sophat, a 20-month-old boy living in Koak Roka village in Siem Reap province in northwest Cambodia.

He was left behind by his parents when he was only 18 months old. The parents traveled to Thailand in search of work and asked the grandfather, Um Oeung, to care for their son.

After the mother left and the boy stopped breast-feeding, he became ill and malnourished – until he noticed a calf nursing from its mother. The boy decided to try suckling and has done so ever since that day.

Grandfather Um Oeung pulled the boy away at first. He relented after his grandson cried piteously and the boy was allowed to continue

suckling.

Villagers found it somewhat uncommon and tried to advice the grandfather but the grandfather expressed his inability to stop his grandson.

He feels that Tha Sophat's health is fine, he is strong and seems to be better off than most other children in the village.

This child is practically surviving on the cow's milk, hardly eating or drinking anything else. The cow doesn't seem to mind it at all also.

Boy Nursing From Cow - Beautiful or Disturbing?

The photos have been circulating around the Internet and many people have called them "disgusting," "unprintable," "unhygienic." It is understandable why the photos might make some people uncomfortable because a child suckling from a cow is an unusual sight. But these photos are simply unusual, not disgusting. This is a beautiful story except for the people who are used to seeing cows as hamburgers and drinking industrialized milk. The poor boy was abandoned by his mother. He

was starving and missed the comfort of suckling. He made an impressive cognitive leap from mother's breast to cow's udder and as a result he's enjoying fresh, raw milk. His health is a testimonial that what he is doing is right.

Those who have never lived with a real cow or tasted real milk, for them it may be hard to understand this personal and intimate account. Milk from factory farms can only be described as white blood where cows are artificially inseminated and given hormones to produce 100 pounds of milk a day. This is several times more than they would produce naturally. As a result, a huge percentage of dairy cows suffer from mastitis, a bacterial infection of the udders. Since this milk is still considered drinkable, the blood and pus from their infections, along with massive quantities of antibiotics, ends up in the milk on supermarket shelves. Many times milk turns pink when blood gets mixed with the milk due to infections and over milking by machines. This milk is turned natural white by adding chemical whiteners.

The minute you start to process your milk, you destroy Mother Nature's perfect food. You can live exclusively on raw milk, especially milk from nature's sacred animal, the cow. We have no sense of the sacredness of our animals today. Instead, we have an industrial system of agriculture that puts our dairy cows inside on cement all their lives and gives them foods that cows are not designed to eat—grain, soy, citrus peel cake and bakery waste. These modern cows produce huge amounts of watery milk which is very low in fat.

Milk from these industrial cows is then shipped to a milk factory. Emily Green wrote an excellent article in the *LA Times*, August 2000 about milk processing. Milk processing plants are big, big factories where visitors are not allowed. Lots can go wrong in these factories. The largest milk poisoning in American history occurred in 1985 where more than 197,000 people across three states were sickened after a "pasteurization failure" at an Illinois bottling plant.

"Who was the first guy that look at a cow and said," I think that I'll drink whatever comes out of those things when I squeeze them?"
—*Calvin & Hobbes*

Inside the plants all you can see is stainless steel. Inside that machinery, milk shipped from the farm is completely remade. First it is separated in centrifuges into fat, protein and various other solids and liquids. Once segregated, these are reconstituted to set levels for whole, low-fat and no-fat milks; in other words, the milk is reconstituted to be completely uniform. The butterfat left over will go into butter, cream, cheese, toppings and ice cream. The dairy industry loves to sell low fat milk and skim milk because they can make a lot more money from the butterfat when consumers buy it as ice cream. When they remove the fat to make reduced fat milks, they replace the fat with powdered milk concentrate, which is formed by high temperature spray drying. All reduced-fat milks have dried skim milk added to give them body, although this ingredient is not usually on the labels. The result is a very high-protein, lowfat product. Because the body uses up many nutrients to assimilate protein—especially the nutrients contained in animal fat—such doctored milk can quickly lead to nutrient deficiencies.

The milk is then pasteurized at 161 degrees F by rushing it past superheated stainless steel plates. If the temperature is 200 degrees the milk is called ultrapasteurized. This will have a distinct cooked milk taste but it is sterile and can be sold on the grocery shelf. In other words, they don't even have to keep it cool. The bugs won't touch it. It does not require refrigeration. As it is cooked, the milk is also homogenized by a pressure treatment that breaks down the fat globules so the milk won't separate. Once processed, the milk will last for weeks and months, not just days.

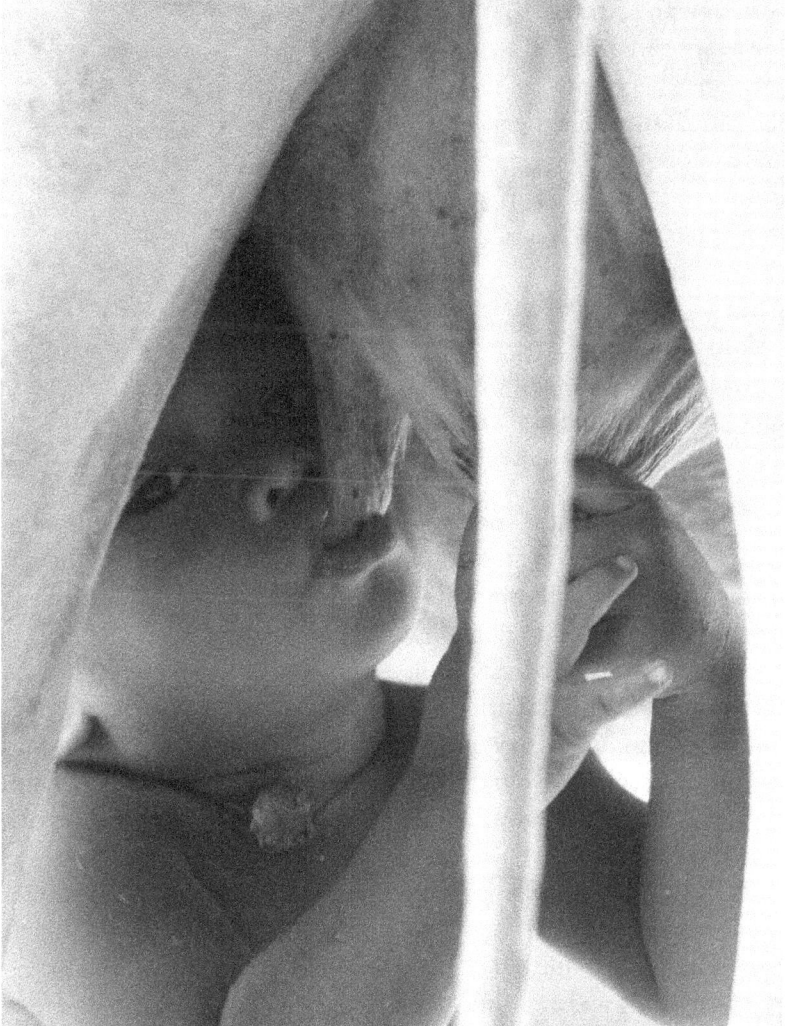

Milk Allergies

Many people, particularly our children, cannot tolerate the stuff that we are calling milk that is sold in the grocery shelves. And you can see why. It starts with cows in confinement, cows fed feed that cows are not designed to digest, and then it goes into these factories for dismantlement and reconfiguration.

The protein compounds in milk have many important roles, including protection against pathogens, enhancement of the immune system and carrier systems for nutrients. However, like the proteins in grains, the proteins in milk are complex, three-dimensional molecules that are very fragile. The pasteurization process deforms and denatures these proteins. When we drink pasteurized milk, the body mounts an immune response instead of deriving instant nourishment.

Real Milk

Real milk is nature's perfect life-giving food which builds strong bone, healthy organs and a strong nervous system. But it is illegal in many countries to sell fresh milk, called raw milk. Many farmers are languishing in jails for selling fresh, raw milk.

Humans consumed raw milk exclusively prior to the industrial revolution and the invention of the pasteurization process in 1864. During the industrial revolution large populations congregated into urban areas detached from the agricultural lifestyle. Up until that point, individuals and families owned their own cows, goats and other livestock and milked them on a daily basis.

Pasteurization was first used in the United States in the 1890s after the discovery of germ theory to control the hazards of contagious bacterial diseases. Initially after the scientific discovery of bacteria, no product testing was available to determine if a farmer's milk was safe or

8

infected, so all milk was treated as potentially contagious.

Regulation of the commercial distribution of packaged raw milk varies across the world. Some countries like Canada, Australia and most parts of US have complete bans, but many have partial bans that do not restrict the purchase of raw milk bought directly from the farmer.

For example, Food and Drug Regulations Act, 1991 of Canada says, "No person shall sell the normal lacteal secretion obtained from the mammary gland of the cow, genus Bos, or of any other animal, or sell a

> *pita-mata mari' khao——eba kon dharma*
> *kon bale kara tumi e-mata vikarma*

"Since the bull and cow are your father and mother, how can you kill and eat them? What kind of religious principle is this? On what strength are you so daring that you commit such sinful activities?"

Everyone can understand that we drink the milk of cows and take the help of bulls in producing agricultural products. Therefore, since our real father gives us food grains and our mother gives us milk with which to live, the cow and bull are considered our father and mother. According to Vedic civilization, there are seven mothers, of which the cow is one. Therefore Sri Chaitanya Mahaprabhu challenged the Muslim Kazi, "What kind of religious principle do you follow by killing your father and mother to eat them?" In any civilized human society, no one would dare kill his father and mother for the purpose of eating them. Therefore Sri Chaitanya Mahaprabhu challenged the system of Muslim religion as patricide and matricide. In the Christian religion also, a principal commandment is "Thou shalt not kill." Nevertheless, Christians violate this rule; they are very expert in killing and in opening slaughterhouses. In our Krishna consciousness movement, our first provision is that no one should be allowed to eat any kind of flesh. It does not matter whether it is cows' flesh or goats' flesh, but we especially stress the prohibition against cows' flesh because according to sastra the cow is our mother. Thus the Muslims' cow-killing was challenged by Sri Chaitanya Mahaprabhu .

—Srila Prabhupada (Sri Chaitanya Charitamrta, Adi 17.154)

dairy product made with any such secretion, unless the secretion or
dairy product has been pasteurized by being held at a temperature and
for a period that ensure the reduction of the alkaline phosphatase activity
so as to meet the tolerances specified in official method MFO-3,
Determination of Phosphatase Activity in Dairy Products, dated
November 30, 1981."

Lucky for us, the boy Tha Sophat was born in Cambodia and not in
Canada, US or Australia. Otherwise state would have taken him away
for indulging in this despicable illegal activity.

*125 years ago, W.D. Hoard, founder of one of the oldest
and well known dairy magazines, penned a tribute to
the dairy cow and recognized the dairy cow as being
the foster mother of the human race when he wrote:
"The cow is the foster mother of the human race. From
the time of the ancient Hindoo to this time have the
thoughts of men turned to this kindly and beneficent creature as one
of the chief sustaining forces of the human race" – W.D. Hoard
As a dairyman, I think it would be appropriate to also recognize the
contributions that these foster mothers have made to human society
in this time when we are celebrating Mothers Day*

3.

Flood Heroine

Now A Pampered Princess

This incident took place in Woodville, 130km north of Wellington, New Zealand. This is about a cow named 569 who saved her owner from swirling flood waters. Now more than six years after her dramatic rescue, Cow 569 is leading a somewhat charmed existence.

She grabbed headlines around the world during the floods in February 2004 after her owner, Mrs Riley was swept away by the swollen Manawatu River on the Woodville dairy farm.

Riley clearly remembers the day. The floods at the farm in 2004

were worse than expected. She and husband Keith were aware the river had risen during the night so they moved the cows to higher ground the next morning not realising, in the dark, that the water had come right up to the cowshed.

"They were spooked in the dark, as they must have known the water was there, but I hadn't seen it in the dark. The next thing I know they were all floating, so I shot out to head them off and I ended up floating between them," Riley recalls.

Mrs Riley was hampered by her wet weather gear and gum boots, and members of her herd, who kept swimming over her.

"I drank a fair bit of water and it was foul muck. There was lots of flotsam around and weeds get tangled up in your arms: it was quite exhausting," she says.

She really started to worry when she tried to grab hold of a passing tree, and the top of a fence, but missed both as she was swept away by the current.

"I thought if I was washed into the main river I would be gone," she adds. That was when the farmer spotted her salvation.

"I looked back and saw one of the last cows bearing down on me. As she came closer I threw my arm over her neck, just sort of grabbed her mane. It was so nice feeling her warm body...

"I just laid back and relaxed ... take me on home!"

When they reached solid ground, 30 metres (98 feet) away, they both sat there "puffing, and shaking a little bit".

She was delighted to find most of her cows gathered on higher ground. All but about 15 of her 350-strong herd survived.

The Friesian cow is now in her 16th year, completely unaware of the fuss she caused, and set to "retire gracefully". Her actions during the flood meant Mrs Riley would never be able to bring herself to send Cow 569 to slaughter – even when she stopped producing milk.

Despite it being nearly seven years since the cow became a household name, people still asked about her.

"Everyone says, do we keep her in the bedroom, but no – she's very much a career girl."

Mrs Riley is still unsure about whether Cow 569 appreciates the attention she has gained.

A bout of mastitis put Cow 569 in "semi-retirement" this year, and she now has her own paddock, looking after an adopted calf nicknamed "Brick".

After the rescue, Mrs Riley wrote the bestselling children's book Cow Power about Cow 569, and says the cow not only saved her life, she also helped her discover new opportunities.

"She opened a whole new world for me."

The Rileys plan to get Cow 569 pregnant again, but, for now, the "boss cow" who is an above average producer is taking it easy.

But shouldn't all the cows, or rather all the animals, should share the fate of cow 569. Aren't all cows benefitting us, rendering selfless service to us? Its not just Cow 569 that has saved some one, in fact all cows and bulls, since thousands of years have saved human civilization from starving to death. Before the introduction of fossil fuels, hundred and fifty years ago, bull provided the necessary power to grow food and establish infrastructure. And cow has been supplying milk, the most essential of all foods since time immemorial. We owe these innocent big eyed creatures a lot.

There are lots of crusades around today: Save the Whale, Save the Seal, Save the Endangered Species. That's good... we can't keep killing

animals and expect there to be peace in the world. Actually, there are laws of nature at work here which are inescapable... laws of God which are controlling our lives. And if we're going to make so many campaigns to save this animal and that animal, let's not make campaigns just because they're going extinct. That means we want to save these creatures not out of compassion, not out of mercy, but just because we like to have them around for our own amusement. That shouldn't be the only reason we want to save animals. We should protect the animals because they happen to be God's creatures, first and foremost. We have to realize that wherever there is consciousness, there is a soul present there-whether in a tree, or an insect, or human, or animal-and we have no right to unnecessarily disturb any soul, in any kind of body. We shouldn't even cut down trees unnecessarily. We shouldn't even kill a fly unnecessarily, what to speak of the cow!

Let's face it, of all the creatures that God has put under our dominion here on this earth, no creature is as generous as the cow. Practically speaking, all of us grew up and became strong by the mercy of the cow. It wouldn't be sentimental or crazy to say that in one sense the cow is like our mother. Every one of us was nourished by the cow. Therefore, if we're going to be kind to every creature, let's start with the most generous creature. Let's be grateful. Let's actually show that we have a higher, spiritual awareness. Let's wake up from the nightmare of the most widespread injustice of all.

Don't be fooled by all these fast-talking politicians. Our modern leaders are trying to keep us in darkness and exploit us. Of course they're gonna tell you it's alright to kill the cow-because it's good business for them. Why should they care? Why should they care what your karma is going to be? Why should they care what's going to happen to you? Why should they care about your consciousness-as long as they can get the money out of your pocket? Therefore we must be prepared to struggle, to enlighten people about the real purpose of life, which is spiritual-about the laws of God, which forbid the unnecessary killing of any creature.

And the real leaders are those who are willing to stand up at any cost and tell you these things. Let's give the cows and all innocent beings our protection. We must stand up for the rights of our fellow citizens of the earth who can't stand up for themselves. Let's close the slaughterhouses. Let's boycott the restaurants and supermarkets. Let's speak out. Let's distribute our literature. Let's change people's minds. Let's change people's hearts. Let's save the cow. Don't worry what your neighbor may think-Save the Cow!

So a sensible person is appalled at how human society treats the cow. The sarcastic expression "sacred cow," for example, as well as the expletive "holy cow!" pain us because they evidence a disrespect, deeply rooted in the language itself, the cow's life. Modern civilised man thinks himself too smart, too scientifically advanced, too free from superstition, artificial piety, and notions of transcendence to respect, what to speak of worship, an animal.

But we don't ask you to worship. Fact is, the cow is the mother of human society because she provides milk, which is a delicious and indispensable part of man's diet. How many tons of milk, yogurt, cheese, ice cream, and butter man consumes daily! And yet how many cows are daily led to slaughter? Never mind piety or transcendence. What really matters is something much more down-to-earth, something no civilisation can ignore if it wants to survive for more than a few centuries.

It's called gratitude. In this case gratitude toward a very real mother. And it is intimately connected with other indispensable qualities, like mercy and compassion. How much more men might show civilised gratitude and compassion toward each other if they could show it toward their mother. Animal-killing is not civilised. Cow-killing is indescribably base.

So leave the cow worship to us. You need to work on preliminaries like respect for your mother and gratefulness for how she feeds you.
— Mathuresa Dasa

I even saw a five-legged cow, that was far holier than those from my farm in Australia. I have developed a strange relationship with cows after being in North India, where the Brahmin bulls stand taller than me – and I'm 6 foot 3! I'd grown on a cattle farm in Australia where the black cows we knew were terrified of us from birth, it was amazing to be able to touch and feed these holy beasts as they nonchalantly stood in the middle of the chaotic roads. They really are more intelligent than I'd guessed. The cows in Australia know that they are food, and yet here they are Gods – and again they know it. — Mark Rodriguez (Devonport, Australia)

4.

Science of Subtle, Non-Verbal Communication

By Kurma Rupa Dasa

After working with cows in close proximity for twelve years I'm convinced that substantial telepathic communication takes place among them. Likewise I'm convinced that cows send thoughts to humans as well and if we tune into the right frequency, we can effectively receive non-verbal messages from them.

A recent example: A street bull I know well entered the small garden to be served. That cold morning I offered him hay sprinkled with hot ginger tea, gur (jaggery), flour and bran, a mixture he most relishes. After consuming his fill, he sniffed the ground and found a suitable

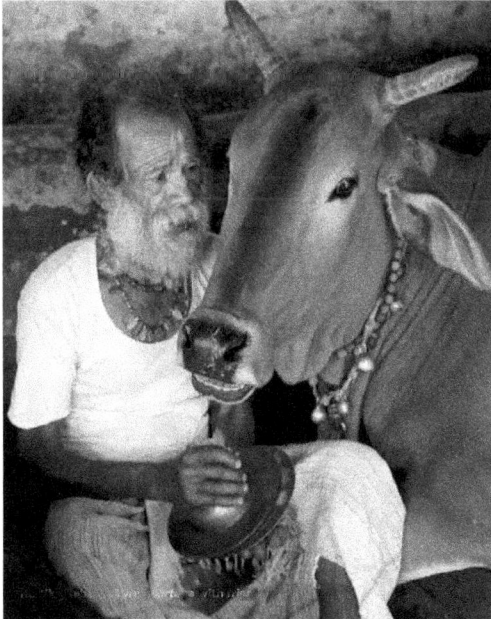

place to sit and ruminate. I sat next to him to chant japa and relish his peaceful company. I thought, "How fortunate am I that I can serve Dharma (religion) Personified in Vrindavan."

The thought he sent me was, "I am grateful to you for that wonderful meal. I especially liked the tidbits of ginger and gur as it takes the chill out of this winter morning."

5.

Brazilian Cow Braves Crocodile Field

Lucky cow! This daring Brazilian cow was spotted moving around fearlessly among crocodiles in search of some tasty treats. Crocodiles, a whole bunch of them, simply looked at her with their mouths wide open, may be in disbelief at her audacity.

Showing the confidence of a catwalk model, but may be with more than a hint of udder idiocy, the barmy Brazilian bovine avoided stepping on the crocs in her search for a good meal.

This brave moo was lucky, the only snap she suffered when wandering into a field full of carnivores was from a camera.

Photographer Robert Mooney, of Arlington, Virginia, took the incredible photograph on the tropical Pantanal swamps in the western state of Mato Grosso.

The 50-year-old said: 'I was amazed the cow dared to stroll among the crocodiles with such apparent ease.'

At the time of report it was not know if she had befriended the colony of crocodiles.

The Pantanal is the world's largest wetland area - covering 88,803 square miles - an area nearly the same size as Scotland.

It stretches to Paraguay in the south, Bolivia in the west, and is home to more than 3,500 species of plants, 650 different kinds of bird and 400 species of fish.

(By Lee Moran, 30th July 2011)

Come to the spiritual platform, brahma-bhutah prasannatma na socati na... [Bg. 18.54], samah sarvesu bhutesu. Then you can see equally. Otherwise you will see that "I have become human being. I have got my hands and legs, and the poor cow has no hands and legs. I have soul and she has no soul. Kill her and eat." No. Samah sarvesu bhutesu. Asamata. Unequality. Why? What right you have got to kill another animal? Because you have no vision of equality, for want of Krsna consciousness. Therefore so-called education, culture, fraternity, in this material world, all these are bogus, humbug.

— *Srila Prabhupada (Lecture, Bhagavad-gita 2.13, London, August 19, 1973)*

6.

The Bull Star

Busier Than Bollywood Heroes

Gopal, a14 year-old bull from Sanosra village in Kutch district in India has dates booked till 2013. He has already mated 486 times, and packs in a busy schedule, with interested parties from as far as Haryana having to book a 'mating appointment.'

And some think that only Bollywood stars have their dates packed for the next two years!

He has a topnotch mating record and is in demand all over Gujarat,

Punjab and Haryana. According to the Gaushala (cow shelter) trustees, Gopal is available by appointment-only system. In last eight months, his schedule has been extremely tight. People coming from far off areas have been camping in the village with their cows.

The reason Gopal is in heavy demand is because he begets 'powerful offsprings.' He has fathered many illustrious sons and daughters. His sons are becoming powerful bulls and his daughters are yielding 15 to 17-litre milk yield per day, much higher than regular cows.

While the average bull tends to mate about 50 times in his lifetime, Gopal has already impregnated 486 cows. And he still has another seven years of his mating cycle to go.

Gopal arrived at the Sanosra Gaushala five and a half years ago when a Kutchi gentleman based in Australia gifted Gopal to the gaushala, impressed by the work they were doing. Gopal was picked up because of his ancestry which can be traced to the Gir cow, belonging to a famous milk cattle breed of India found in the Gir hills of Gujarat and the forests of Kathiawar.

Like every busy star, Gopal gets off time too — twice every year, around June and December.

The reason for such scarcity of good bulls is simple to understand. In the last 250 years, there was a deliberate attempt to break the backbone of a nation and subjugate it by destroying its economic fabric.

India had the world's best draught animals, particularly oxen. They were promoted in pre-Independence India by princely states and temple trusts, which provided funds to develop specialised breeds as well as stud bulls for breed improvement in villages.

Of India's over 100 known cattle breeds, most were developed for draught in times when the economy ran on animal power. With the Green Revolution, it was assumed tractors would make draught animals irrelevant. Government support for breed maintenance died out. So much so, most indigenous cattle '80-90 percent' is now categorised as 'non-descript'.

This trail of destruction in fact began with the arrival of the British in the middle of the 18th century in India. India was known all over the world for her immense wealth and a highly advanced culture. Cows formed the backbone of it and cows were such an inseparable part of its daily life that Indian culture of that period can safely be termed as cow culture.

When the British colonized India, they studied India thoroughly to keep her under subjugation. Robert Clive, the Governor of British India at the time, made an extensive research in Indian economic and agricultural systems. He found that Indian society was firmly footed in its age-old customs and sound economic and agricultural practices, all based on cow protection. We can quote a letter of Lord MCLau here, a British colonial dated February 2, 1835.

"I have traveled across the length and breath of India and I have not seen one person who is a beggar, who is a thief, such wealth I have seen in this country, such high moral values, people of such caliber (of noble character), that I do not think we would ever conquer this country...........unless we break the very backbone of this nation which is her spiritual and cultural heritage."

So during his surveys, Robert Clive found that in 1740, in the Arcot District of Tamil Nadu, 54 Quintals of rice was harvested from one acre of land using manure and pesticides made from cow urine and cow dung. Cow was the foundation of this great nation and cows greatly outnumbered men. He realized that unless this foundation was shaken up, they could not keep their hold on India for too long. This inspired him to open the first ever slaughterhouse in Indian in 1760, with a capacity to kill thousands of cows every week. As a part of the master

So Radha-kunda Mukerjee, he has supported cow slaughter. He was given a post, made a parliament member first of all. So this poor man, five hundred rupees per month, he accepted. Then he induced that "You take more money, write like this." So if you pay money... British government's whole policy was that if the Indians are kept strict Hindus, it is next to impossible to govern them. So therefore they adopted this policy. They changed the whole policy how the Hindu will think everything mentioned in the sastra is nonsense. They have trained up, and Nehru is the first-class trainee.

—Srila Prabhupada (Room Conversation, Vrindavan, March 12, 1972)

plan to destabilize India, cow slaughter was initiated. To this extent, the British were quite successful. Cow slaughter, engineered by them, divided Hindu and Muslim communities which had coexisted peacefully for the last 700 years. Millions died in ensuing riots which lasted for decades. To this day, India and Pakistan are locked in bitter enemity and continuously suffering.

Robert Clive started a number of slaughter houses before he left India. By 1910, 350 slaughterhouses were working day and night. India was reduced to severe poverty, millions were dying from hunger and malnutrition, age-old cottage industries were devastated and village artisans took up jobs as coolies in cities. Manchester cloth effectively destroyed Indian handlooms and textiles enterprise. Using Indian money and Indian man power, the British were expanding their empire all over the world.

Bereft of its cattle wealth, India had to approach England for industrial manure. Thus industrial manure like urea and phosphate made way to India. Indian villages, in which once flowed streams of milk and butter, became haunted hamlets, wretched and starving. A Paradise was lost. An India where horses and bullocks were made to drink ghee, was now suffering from scarcity of margarine. It was total devastation of a great civilization.

The British established an educational system which decried anything connected with Indian tradition. This was a crafty engineering by Macaulay who said, "We must at present do our best to form a class of persons Indian in blood and colour but English in tastes, in opinion, in morals, and in intellect." He did this so effectively that even after sixty years of independence Indians still continue to exist in a state of stupor, unable (and even unwilling!) to extricate themselves from one of the greatest hypnoses woven over a whole nation.

By the time British departed from India, thousands of slaughterhouses were in operation and now its hard to keep a count of them. The result is this - 40000 suicides by Indian farmers every year and the largest number of malnourished children in the World.

23

7.

Secret of India's Street Roaming Cows
By Lin Shujuan (China Daily)

Chaotic, loud, hot and crowded. Diverse, charming and full of stories. There are as many Indias as there are travelers to that country.

It is often said that you'll either love India or hate it. I disagree. You can only love it in the way you love chocolate. You might get sick from a temporary sensory overload, but its temptation is a lasting one.

Before I set out, I knew little about India. I couldn't even tell the difference between Hinduism and Buddhism. My knowledge about the country was restricted to some contacts with Indian friends, an occasional peek at online photos posted by tourists and the beautiful TV commercial of Incredible India.

I had intentionally not prepared much for the trip except for picking up medicine to protect my stomach against the infamous Delhi belly. Travel has always been one of the best ways to learn about another culture and country. I preferred to keep it that way.

The five-day trip was such a cultural treat that three weeks later, I am still talking about it with colleagues and friends and, even more surprising, they are still interested.

Like most first-time travelers to the country, my two friends and I chose the tried and tested Golden Triangle route, comprising New Delhi, Agra and Jaipur. But we got little time to see around Delhi because travel between the three cities took up much of our time and energy, the latter dissipating rather quickly in the heat of temperatures 30 C

and above.

For someone ignorant of India, like me, culture shock hit the moment we got on the road from Delhi to Agra.

Buses, cars, trucks, scooters, auto-rickshaws, bicycles, pedestrians - and animals - share the roads, paying scant attention to traffic rules. Some buses run with their doors missing. Auto-rickshaws are packed with passengers not just inside, but on their roofs. Trucks seem to take a more polite approach, with each of them carrying this sign on their rear bumpers - Blow Horn!

However, once you get used to the chaos, you sense an underlying harmony. Our guide is very helpful telling us how to distinguish between different religious groups from the way they dress, and what their religious differences are all about.

India you will find in the bazaars. There is crowd, and the cows enter there, and they eat the vegetables to their heart's content. But she is not punishable. Still the cow is not punishable. Maximum a stick will be shown. But if a man takes one potato without the permission, he is punishable, he will be sent to jail.
— *Srila Prabhupada (Lecture, Srimad-Bhagavatam 6.1.39, San Francisco, July 20, 1975)*

Seeing all these different people share the street peacefully with one another - besides an assortment of animals including cows, sheep, monkeys, pigs and even squirrels - I come to appreciate India's cultural cohesiveness.

I'm also fascinated by the sight of cows wandering the streets, navigating the traffic with great ease.

It isn't difficult to understand why Indians would allow cows to stroll on the streets, but I couldn't quite figure out why the cows would enjoy the outing. That question lingered in my mind till the end of the trip.

I ran into a pair of twin sisters from Britain at the airport while heading back to Beijing. I finally solved the riddle of the cows on the roads. They told me why the cows liked to stroll or even just stand on the streets - the busy traffic kept mosquitoes and flies away from their bodies! That was a cool way to keep pests away, I thought.

A five-day trip is simply too short for a country like India. I have to go back there, many times.

A disciple has read an article from government side that in Iran they want meat, so all these skinny cows should be killed and meat should be exported so that you can get oil economically. So one should not think of this religious sentiment. They should be practical. They should not object. Government is going to open many slaughterhouse to get oil, and kill these loitering, mischief loitering cows who have no food. Like that. So government policy is that religion is an opiate of the masses. It is a sentiment. It has no value. That is government conclusion.
— Srila Prabhupada (Room Conversation, March 20, 1974, Bombay)

A Universal Friend

Today there are about 1.5 billion cows in the world. In many different countries humans and cows have formed close relationships. In England, dairy farmer Mark Evans spends all of his waking time with his cows, milking, feeding, and otherwise nurturing them. The African Masai tribe believes that all cattle were given to them from the great god N'gai at the beginning of time - a belief which today remains at the heart of their culture. India is home to a quarter of the world's cow population. One major reason for this is that India's majority Hindu community reveres cows and considers them to be "second mothers."

8.

Beat Stress, Rent A Cow

What best to combat the stress of city life than renting a placid Swiss cow? This is the serious offer made by a farmer in the Alpine country, who claims that fresh air and a new ruminant friend can help city-dwellers regain serenity.

Most Swiss head to the beaches for their vacations, but others are opting for a rustic holiday in the mountains where they are spending time with their adopted cows over the summer.

Launched five years ago by herder Michel Izoz, a cow adoption project called Mavachamoi — word play in French for "my cow" — is proving popular among urban dwellers in Switzerland.

Among the 20 cows available for rent at his farm in La Lecherette in the canton Vaud, only Ilda, Rosette, Tola, Ursula, Usine and Quenele are still available. All the others have been booked for the summer.

Izoz noted that some cows are more popular than others, especially those with horns as they "appear more authentic."

Clients go online to the website www.mavachamoi.ch for a catalogue showcasing the cows on postcard perfect meadows. For 280 euros, they

"I never met a cow I didn't like."
—*Jennie Garth*

can reserve a cow for a season, during which they can visit the animal as often as they wish.

The project offers a chance for city dwellers to compare "the stressed out world of the cities and the hard lives in the mountains."

Izoz says that he had started the project mainly to "show people that farming life is really different from what we imagine."

To put forward his point, Izoz requires clients to spend at least four hours working at the farm, during which they are to round up the herd, cut wood, participate in the treatment or making of cheese prepared in wood fire in the large copper vats.

"Often, it makes my son laugh" to see the city people doing the farm work that requires some dexterity, says Esther Ginier, another farmer who offers 16 cows for rent at her farm in La Comballaz.

There is no room for stress in the idyllic mountain pastures where work is seven days a week and where one has to live with nature and its rules.

The adoption also offers other surprises.

The children discover in Switzerland, the country of cows, that milk does not come from packets. Straight from the udder, it's smooth, it's warm, it's sweet.

Parents meanwhile also manage to revisit their childhood memories. They also often leave with farm products.

They realise that "the cows are not that dumb and that like people, they have their own character, with a dominant one, a curious one, a greedy one... and even nasty ones which charge at them.

Claude Kobler has adopted Sirene since 2007. For him, it is about making a contribution to the alpine herders.

But what makes the IT consultant of a Geneva bank happy is the contact with the different world.

His Fribourgeouis speckled cow appears to enjoy the patronage too, "as it produces more and more milk."

The devout cowboy lost his favorite Bible while he was mending fences out on the range. Three weeks later, a cow walked up to him carrying the Bible in its mouth. The cowboy couldn't believe his eyes. He took the precious book out of the cow's mouth, raised his eyes heavenward and exclaimed, "It's a miracle!" "Not really," said the cow. "Your name is written inside the cover."

9.

'Sweet' Memories of World War II

Easter week always reminds Bela J. Bognar of his young life in western Hungary, World War II, and "a cow named Sandy."

Bognar, the father of award-winning filmmaker Steve Bognar, lives in Casstown, in Miami County these days, and he tells a captivating story.

It all happened Easter week in 1945 when Bognar was 13 years old and the war was winding down. His memory is still vivid of the days when Russian soldiers took over the small Hungarian village where he lived with his family.

"This one morning there were lots of strange noises. When the fog cleared we found there were literally thousands of Russian soldiers in the area. They were ransacking homes and looking for German soldiers and arms."

He remembers crying when he saw that the invaders set fire to his school building, a Catholic school that had, "the largest library in the region."

His village had about a thousand residents, and he said the women, about half the population, fled to hiding places in the nearby hills as "the Russian soldiers raved, raped and stole."

German soldiers, who preceded the Russians, had taken cows from several villages and loaded them into railroad cars.

"On the Tuesday after Easter I saw her for the first time," he said. "She was a beautiful cow attached at the neck by a thick rope to a

32

wagon. When I saw her I knew I must have her. But how?"

"I approached the young Russian (in charge of the cow) and said 'chen-chen' and pointed to the cow. Chen-chen was a universal word for changing, or exchanging."

The Russian soldiers were "obsessed" with wristwatches, and this one called out 'chasy'. "We all knew that meant a 'watch.'

Something clicked and Bognar told the young warrior, "Chasy? Da, da, doma," which means 'yes, yes, home.'

Bognar ran to his home in the village and pulled an antique watch out of a dresser drawer where it had long been stored. When you wound the watch it would run for 10 minutes, then stop and would need rewinding.

He continued, "I grabbed it, wound it, and ran back. The herd was on its way, but the soldier waited for me. I handed him the watch and he listened to it ticking, and put it in his bag. He had wristwatches on both of his arms. He smiled and pointed to the cow."

At that point Bognar took the bloody rope off the cow's neck. "I hugged her and said in Hungarian 'gyere velem' or 'follow me.' "

"I did not look back. She followed me all the way home to our barn where there was plenty of hay. I hugged her again and whispered, 'You are mine.'

His parents rushed to the barn to see the prize that young Bela had brought home.

"We named her Sandy because of her beautiful fawn color. She had a calf each year, and continued to provide plenty of milk. When I finally left Hungary in 1956, Sandy was still the pride and joy of the family."

(By Dale Huffman for Daily News)

The words of Lord Chaitanya Mahaprabhu, the greatest authority, herein clearly indicate that one becomes pious simply by keeping cows and protecting them. Unfortunately, people have become such rascals that they do not even care about the words of an authority. People generally consider cowherd men lowly members of society, but herein Caitanya Mahaprabhu confirms that they are so pious......Heeding this instruction by the Lord, people should serve cows and calves and in return get ample quantities of milk. There is no loss in serving the cows and calves, but modern human society has become so degraded that instead of giving protection to the cows and serving them, people are killing them. How can they expect peace and prosperity in human society while committing such sinful activities? It is impossible.
—Srila Prabhupada (Sri Chaitanya Charitamrta, Adi 17.111)

10.

Cows Turn Pastureland Into Useful Food

By Bill Croushore

One of the perks of my career is the opportunity to work outside in the springtime. The grass is getting green and the weather is getting warmer and all seems right with the world. As we get later into spring, many of the dairy cattle will get the opportunity to go outside the barn and eat some grass.

While the grass isn't tall enough yet to allow for substantial grazing, it is getting there. Ruminants, like the cow, are specially adapted to eat grass and turn it into energy and protein. This is made possible by the rumen, the large fermentation chamber of the cow's complex stomach.

When a cow eats grass, the bacteria, yeast and protozoa organisms in her rumen are able to convert the otherwise indigestible parts of the grass into energy and protein the cow can use. The dairy cow uses the energy and protein to manufacture milk in the udder.

Because in India still the system is a householder keeps at least, in the village, at least ten to twelve cows. But he hasn't got to pay anything for keeping these. The cows go to the pasturing ground and in the evening comes back. And some grass, dry grass which is by-product of the grains, that is offered to her, and instead of, in place she offers milk. So milk in the village, still it is available very easily, without any expenses.

—Srila Prabhupada (Lecture, Bhagavad-gita 3.17-20, New York, May 27, 1966)

When a cow takes a bite of grass, she doesn't waste much time in chewing it; that might interfere with her next bite of grass. Instead, she swallows it then takes another bite and she will worry about chewing later.

After a lengthy time spent grazing, the cow will eventually lie down and chew her cud. Her complex stomach will sort the feed she has already ingested into that which needs chewed and that which has already been.

I know it sounds disgusting. Chewing food that has already been eaten; I must be kidding, right? It would most certainly be disgusting if the cow wasn't a ruminant, but she is and she most certainly enjoys it. I have never seen an animal more content than a cow chewing her cud.

To the cow, chewing her cud is heaven on earth. When she chews her cud, she grinds the fibrous feed material into a pulp so that the microorganisms in her rumen can do the work of digesting it. Without the process, the grass couldn't be digested.

When the cow swallows her cud, it goes back to the rumen to be mixed and sloshed around to ensure complete digestion. Then, the remainder passes out of the rumen to finish the digestion process.

You may notice as you see the cows grazing this spring that they are

allelomimetic. That means each animal does the same thing as those nearby. Social animals display this behaviour. When cows graze, they are either all standing and grazing, or all lying down and chewing their cud, with the exception of some cows that have anti-establishment tendencies.

We really should be thankful for cows for their ability to take otherwise useless grass and turn it into food for people. It has been said that cows are the foster mothers of the human race and I have to believe that is true.

(Dr. Croushore is a veterinarian with White Oak Veterinary Clinic in Berlin, Germany.)

11.

Fresh Grass to Fresh Milk

A Life Giving Miracle

U nless you have studied animal biology you have probably wondered how a cow produces milk from grass? This is how it works.

Unlike most mammals the cow has four stomachs not just one, the rumen, the reticulum, the omasum, and the abomasums.

When a cow grazes grass or eats other fodder she swallows it half chewed and it goes to the first stomach, the rumen. In the rumen digestive fluids and bacteria soften the grass and when it is ready it moves naturally to the second stomach, the reticulum.

In the reticulum the grass is formed into small lumps called cuds.

Acintya-sakti, inconceivable power. The cow, eating grass, producing milk—this is inconceivable power. Can you produce milk from the grass? But how the cow is producing? Hmm? Answer this. You eat grass and produce milk. Give your wife grass and let her produce milk. It is God's desire. Cow is eating dry grass and producing the nicest thing, milk, full of vitamins. Now, if you think, "Oh, then dry grass and straw contain all vitamins. Let me eat," you will die. You will die. It is God's arrangement.
— Srila Prabhupada (Morning Walk, April 3, 1975, Mayapur)

After awhile these cuds return to the mouth and the cow then chews each for about one or so minutes. When the cud is swallowed it goes to the third stomach, the omasum.

In the omasum the cud is broken down and nutrients from the grass are absorbed into the blood stream of the cow. The remaining cud then passes to the fourth and final stomach, the abomasums.

In the abomasums grass is broken down even further by digestive fluids and from there it passes into the intestine, where the nurishment continues to be absorbed into the blood stream.

In the cows udder is where the final miracle of milk making takes place. The udder has four identical sections and each section has a teat. In the udder the cow process her blood and transforms it into nutritious milk.

The transformation of fresh grass to fresh milk is indeed a life giving miracle.

12.

Basava - An Oracle Ox

Mad Cow vs. Sacred Cow

The rural hamlet of Chikka Arasinakere in the South Indian state of Karnataka is run by an ox named Basava. Not exactly landlord or mayor; more like an oracle. All major decisions, public or private, are put to Basava and he handles them so judiciously that his fame has spread throughout South India. Bus-loads of devotees now arrive from afar to consult the sacred ox.

Judging from the look of the tidy little village - with its few hundred households, its fields of sugar cane and millet, its temple, ritual purification tank and fringe of collectively owned grazing lands - Basava runs Chikka Arasinakere pretty well. No wonder: He's been at it for

nearly 800 years over the course of 25 incarnations. Acolytes identify each successive Basava through a system of dreams and portents, a process akin to finding a new Dalai Lama.

Basava gets handsomely paid for his oracular services. Jasmine and marigolds garland his massive neck and hump. A richly ornamented silver bangle bedecks his right front hoof — the hoof with which he signals his 'yea' or 'nay' to any question posed. His 30-inch horns are strung with fat bundles of cash, up to a million rupees' worth (about $21,000) at a time, which are harvested every week or so.

So this is a civilization of killing father and mother. All over the world they are killing bulls and cows. In England there is law that you can maintain a cow but you cannot maintain a bull. It must be killed. Yes. When I was a guest in John Lennon's house the manager in charge, he was telling me. "You cannot keep bull. This is our law." I learned from him.

Hari-Sauri: Only for breeding purposes. Only for breeding. All the rest are killed.

Prabhupada: This is law in England? So you cannot keep even bull privately. Must be killed. This is the law.

Tamala Krsna: What is the reason for that law?

Prabhupāda: Bull will not supply milk, so there is no use. It must be killed. You have made this law. The cows may be given some time to be killed, but the bulls should be killed immediately. This is their law.

Hari-sauri: Nor do the farmers actually want to keep them anyway. For them, they are useless animals.

Prabhupada: Simply expensive. But here in India they know how to utilize bulls—for transportation, for plowing and so many other things.

Tamala Krsna: Such a shortage of fuel, but there is no shortage of fuel with a bull.

Prabhupada: No, rather, it will supply you gobar, fuel. Whatever he will eat, he will give you fuel.

— Srila Prabhupada (Morning Walk, February 3, 1976, Mayapura)

The donors of these rupees get value for money, according to a list of Basava's "miracles" in a pamphlet distributed at his shrine. The ox has been known to cure diseases, dowse wells, find buried treasures, arrange marriages, arbitrate disputes, catch thieves, exorcise demons, render barren couples fertile, ordain priests, survey boundaries, audit financial accounts, convert atheists, purge "witches" and boost exam scores.

It's not as though every bovine in India performs such feats. Nor does every village boast an oracle ox of its own. But cows, as a species, do provide an array of more modest bounties central to the web of traditional rural life.

The bull is the emblem of the moral principle, and the cow is the representative of the earth. When the bull and the cow are in a joyful mood, it is to be understood that the people of the world are also in a joyful mood. The reason is that the bull helps production of grains in the agricultural field, and the cow delivers milk, the miracle of aggregate food values. The human society, therefore, maintains these two important animals very carefully so that they can wander everywhere in cheerfulness. But at the present moment in this age of Kali both the bull and the cow are now being slaughtered and eaten up as foodstuff by a class of men who do not know the brahminical culture.

— *Srila Prabhupada (Srimad Bhagavatam 1.16.18)*

13.
We Are A Family

The kingdom of Vijayanagaram in south India was ruled by King Krishnadeva Raya. One day an old lady and her grown up son visited him in the court. The king respectfully received the lady, addressing her as Daima.

His courtier Tenali Raman noticed him addressing her as such and wondered why he did so. He could not help asking the king about it. The king replied that she nursed him in his childhood and therefore he treated her as his mother and called her Daima. Daima had a son whom the king affectionately addressed as his 'dear half-brother'. They struck

up a rapport right away and this half-brother started hanging around with the king.

The king started spending a lot of time with his half-brother and at times he would not even visit the court. The state administration was getting neglected. The courtiers did not like so much attention to be showered upon the old woman and her son and eagerly wanted them to depart. One day finally when they had left, the king said to Tenali Raman, "You know, I had such a good time in the company of my half-brother. I don't think you have one, otherwise you would have known the warmth of brotherly love."

Tenali Raman replied, "Your Majesty, I too have a half-brother." This claim surprised the king because every one knew Tenali Raman was the only child of his parents. The king asked him to bring his half-brother to the court so that every one can see him.

Tenali Raman hesitated and tried to put it off for a few days. But when the king insisted, Tenali Raman one day arrived in the court with a rope in his hand, with a calf following him. The king was surprised and angrily asked Tenali Raman, "What is the matter with you? Why have you brought a calf in the court?"

Tenali Raman relied, "Your Majesty, this is my half-brother that you wanted to see.

The angry king exclaimed, "What is this joke? I never heard of any one having a calf as a half-brother ?"

Tenali Raman quipped, "Cow is my Daima because she nursed me with her milk. Since she is my foster mother, her son naturally becomes my half-brother."

The entire court burst out laughing and so did the king.

The cow is the mother because just as one sucks the breast of one's mother, human society takes cow's milk. Similarly, the bull is the father of human society because the father earns for the children just as the bull tills the ground to produce food grains. Human society will kill its spirit of life by killing the father and the mother.
—*Srila Prabhupada (Srimad Bhagavatam 3.2.29)*

14.
Bovine Buddies

Cows can make friends and at least one researcher has shown that such bonds among a herd may impact a dairy's bottom line.

Krista McLennan, a researcher and associate lecturer in Animal Welfare, made the discovery while working on her doctoral program involving a study of the social bonds among dairy cattle and the effects of group systems on welfare and productivity at England's Northampton University.

The 27-year-old measured the heart rates and cortisol levels of cows to see how they cope when isolated. Cattle were penned on their own,

with their best friend or with another cow they did not know for 30 minutes and their heart rates were measured at 15-second intervals.

The research showed cows are indeed social animals and often form close connections with other animals in their herd.

When heifers have their preferred partner with them, their stress levels in terms of their heart rates are reduced compared with if they were with a random individual. If we can encourage farmers to keep an eye out for those cows which like to keep their friends with them, it could have some real benefits, such as improving their milk yields and reducing stress for the animals, which is very important for their welfare.

McLennan noted that modern farming practices often means cows are separated during visits from a veterinarian or when farmers move their animals.

"We know re-grouping cows is a problem, because there's a high level of stress among animals as they try to integrate into a new group," she states.

What It All Means

The story of "bovine buddies" has received enormous media exposure, especially considering that it was a doctoral project, not a study authored by seasoned scientists. Earthweek, the environmental news service, covered it in detail. VegNews, a British vegetarian news service, trumpeted the findings under the headline, "Cows get Stressed When Separated." Mainstream media also got involved, with stories syndicated by the *Associated Press*, McClatchy-Tribune News Service also weighed in with reports on the research.

Whenever one has had occasion to visit India, one has invariably found the sacred cows peaceful, far from intimidating and, above all, minding their own business. One is left to wonder why? After all, a cow is a cow is a cow. One supposes the contrast may well be due to the marked difference between the Western and Eastern ethos. Does make one wish the human beings would take a leaf out of the way of life of the bovines! There must be a moral in this somewhere, though one is at a loss to pinpoint it.— Jason Wright, El Paso

Why? Three reasons come to mind:

-*Anthropomorphism.* We modern folk humanize virtually every species in the animal kingdom. Egged on by the endless Disney-fiction of animals, we ascribe (of course, we may be justified in doing so) human-like intelligence, emotions and behaviors to everything from singing, dancing dinosaurs to cats and dogs with more personality than game-show hosts to sharks who swear off eating fish in order to access their nobler selves. Within that contest, cows palling around with buddies in the barn seems as natural as the hay that they're eating.

-*Empathy.* Deep down, almost all of us want food animals treated humanely and given opportunities for a satisfying life. If "friendship" can be part of that package, all the better.

- *Reconnection.* With the cultivation and production of virtually all of our food-supply staples—with the possible exception of some summertime excursions to a u-pick field or farmers' market—divorced and distanced from us urban dwellers, the idea that something simple could leverage a better life for dairy cows provides a pathway for people to feel as if they have informed opinions on the often-complex issues related to food.

All that said, from what has been published, a change in management that would allow cows to spend the bulk of their time with herd mates that seem to keep them calmer makes sense. With all livestock, producers invest heavily in ventilation, lighting and feeding systems designed to reduce stress and improve performance.

Why not a buddy system? If it helps maintain the cows' temperament and contributes to better care, that seems like a sensible strategy to pursue.

And if it helps support the notion that producers are growing more sensitive to animals' emotional and psychological needs, where's the harm in that?

(By Dan Murphy, a veteran food-industry journalist)

> *A cow is another animal that has its own particular aroma. I'm not talking about the stench that overwhelms your smelling orifices when you pass one of our local dairies. I'm talking about the cow's own body odor and breath aroma. It is very special just as a cow's own personal scent. This smell sometimes is triggered if I smell a partly empty milk carton, and remember how many times a cow kicked over a milk bucket when it was almost full, or how annoying it was to get hit in the face with a dirty cow's tail or kicked over backward from an ornery cow's back leg.*
> *—Tony L. Carter*

15.

Brave act

70-year-old Fights off Tiger To Rescue Cow

In a daring act, a 70-year-old shepherd Mangilal of Bhindora village in Madhya Pradesh, central India, fought off a tiger attack just to rescue a cow. Armed with only a bamboo stick, the septuagenarian not only chased away the tiger but also guarded the cows all night long before handing them to their owner. This incident took place in October 2011.

Notably, the beast has already hunted down 27 cattle in the earlier month.

Narrating on how he encountered the tiger in jungles, Mangilal says, "Like always, I had taken my cattle for grazing near the hill top on Sunday. It was 5 in the evening when I halted with the cattle herd near a mine. I rested near the bushes while the cows drank water. The next moment I saw a tiger that crept into the herd and attacked them."

Mangilal took no time to hit the tiger back with his stick. "As soon as the stick hit the tiger, it left the cow. Thinking that it would attack me, I grabbed the axe kept next to me. However, he vanished into the jungle."

In shock after his encounter with the beast for the first time, Mangilal recalls, "I have been rearing cattle since the age of 8 years, but I came across such an experience for the first time. The attack had led to the shattering of the cattle. It was an ordeal to gather them back, for which I had to spend the whole night in jungle."

Not only did Mangilal rescue the cow, the 70-year-old sat next to the injured animal fearing another attack by the tiger. "I thought, the tiger would come back again in search for its prey, but it did not. I handed the injured cow to its owner in the morning."

The injured cow belongs to Sarpanch of Mindora village, Suresh Singh Tomar. The Sarpanch said that the tiger has so far targeted seven cows of their village.

(Source: Bhaskar News)

One who becomes virasana takes the vow to stand all night with a sword to give protection to the cows. Because Prsadhra was engaged in this way, it is to be understood that he had no dynasty. We can further understand from this vow accepted by Prsadhra how essential it is to protect the cows. Some son of a ksatriya would take this vow to protect the cows from ferocious animals, even at night. What then is to be said of sending cows to slaughterhouses? This is the most sinful activity in human society.

— Srila Prabhupada (Srimad Bhagavatam 9.2.3)

16.

The Emotional Depth of A Cow

By Hannah Velten

News that cows have best friends comes as no surprise to those of us who have worked with them – and their mood swings.

Who would think that beneath that calm exterior there is a boiling mass of emotions? I'm not talking about Wimbledon champions here, but cows. Yes, cows; those creatures that we eat, and take milk from, but rarely think about.

In his book The Cow, the former butcher and poet Beat Sterchi invented an adjective to describe the way that cows stand placidly – "cowpeaceably". If you watch cows lying down in a field they will normally be ruminating (chewing on regurgitated grass), staring blankly into space and looking totally at peace. This state of total calmness makes the cow appear withdrawn and "otherworldly". This is perhaps why we assume there is nothing much going on between a cow's ears.

But we cow lovers have always known that cows have emotional depth. DH Lawrence wrote brilliantly about his relationship with Susan, a black cow that he milked every morning in 1924-5 on his ranch in Taos, New Mexico. He comments on her "cowy oblivion", her "cow inertia", her "cowy passivity" and her "cowy peace" and he wonders where she goes to in her trances. But he believes, quite rightly, that there is always "a certain untouched chaos in her", which is never far away. Some days, he writes, she is "fractious, tiresome, and a faggot".

This is because she will deliberately do things to annoy him, such as swinging her tail in his face during milking: "So sometimes she swings it, just on purpose: and looks at me out of the black corner of her great, pure-black eye, when I yell at her."

To anyone who works, or has worked, with cows, it comes as no surprise that cows are capable of friendships. Within any herd there is a pecking order that results in cows coming into the milking parlour every time in more or less the same position in the queue. At the dairy farm I worked on as an agricultural student we had "Devilish Delilah", "Crafty Caroline" and "Pain-In-The-Arse Mary-Rose" – all of which were nicknamed because of their annoying or aggressive antics at milking time or feeding time. Dominant cows will push their way to the front of the queue, bully and intimidate more sensitive souls, and dictate when and where the group will move around their pasture. No submissive cow would want to be their "best friend".

Certain cows will always be the ring leaders when trouble occurs – bulldozing fences until they give way is often found out by accident, but then pursued with great joy by the felons. And woe betide anyone

who gets in the way of a protective mother and her calf; she'll knock you for six and reverse over you for good measure.

Has anyone tried laying down in a field of cows? They will come over and give you a good sniffing and a kindly lick. It's soothing and quite pleasant. Most do exhibit this behaviour, will be curious of any new thing but terrified of it at the same time. The braver ones will come forward to investigate first, but will stand at such a distance that their necks and tongues will be stretched out as far as possible so they don't have to be too close. They will snort, sniff and try to lick the novelty until they decide after about 15 minutes that they are bored and will wander off. There's a lot going on between those hairy ears.

(Hannah Velten is a freelance writer and author who has worked extensively with cattle on British and Australian dairy farms.)

Suppose you are engaged in some work, and if you know that "After seven days, I will be killed," can you do the work very nicely? No. Similarly, the cows know in the Western countries that "These people giving me very nice grains and grass, but after all, they will kill me." So they are not happy. But if they are assured that "You'll not be killed," then they will give double milk, double milk. That is stated in the sastra. During Maharaja Yudhisthira's time, the cows milk bag was so filled up that in the pasturing ground they were dropping, and the whole pasturing ground became moist, muddy with milk. The land used to be muddy with milk, not with water.
— Srila Prabhupada (Srimad-Bhagavatam 6.1.3, Melbourne, May 22, 1975)

17.

Holy Cow That Received Enlightenment

Sri Ramana Maharshi (1879 – 1950), was a monist yogi who lived in the foothills of Arunchala mountain, west of the pilgrimage town Tiruvannamalai in south India.

Every morning the master used to sit for a silent satsanga, communion. He never talked much, unless asked something. Then too his answer was very short. There was no much explanation in it. His literature is confined to two, three small booklets.

Mostly he practiced silent communion with his disciples. Naturally, not many were attracted to him. But every morning he was sitting, people were sitting, and a cow would come and stand outside, putting her neck through the window, and she would remain standing there while the satsanga session lasted. It must have continued for years. People came and went, new people joined, but the cow remained constant... and at the exact time, never late. And as the satsanga would disperse she would go away.

One day she did not appear, and Sri Raman said, "Today satsanga session cannot be held, because my real audience is absent. I am afraid either the cow is very sick or she has died, and I have to go and look for her."

The cow belonged to a poor woodcutter who lived near the ashram. Raman went to the woodcutter and asked, "What happened? The cow has not come today for satsanga."

The woodcutter said, "She is very sick and I am afraid she is dying, but she goes on staring at the door, as if she is waiting for someone.

Perhaps she is waiting for you, to see you for the last time. Perhaps that is why she is staying around a little longer."

Raman went in and there were tears in the eyes of the cow. And she died happily, putting her head in the lap of the master. Ramana declared that she had attained enlightenment and that his disciples should make a beautiful memorial in her honour.

18.

Last Frontiers of Inhumanity

Abuse, Torture And Cruel Death March of India's Sacred Cows

They are supposed to be sacred animals. Revered above all other beasts by Hindus - ranked as high as Brahmin priests, the "twice-born", for their sweetness and generosity - cows still tramp the streets of most Indian towns and cities, mingling with the traffic, nosing through the rubbish skips in the markets, roaming deserted highways at night.

They are huge but very docile. The native breed is creamy white in colour, with a distinctive hump. Sometimes a pious Hindu can be seen feeding a roadside cow with a carrot or chapati. Rarely are they the butt of anger or impatience.

And a fleeting appraisal from the comfort of a tour bus might suggest that India's cows have survived the country's patchy modernisation unscathed. But a campaign launched recently by People for Ethical Treatment of Animals (PETA), backed up by The Independent's own investigation, reveals the Indian treatment of its holiest animal as a scandal of cruelty, greed and corruption.

The cow's special status in India is enshrined in law. With the exception

56

of two states, the slaughter of cows and calves is totally forbidden, whatever the reason and at whatever age. Bulls and bullocks and she-buffaloes are protected up to 15 years of age.

The arrival of Hindu nationalists in power both at the centre, where they were the leading party in a coalition, and in a number of states, also enhanced the protection which cows receive. Between 1995 and 1999, the Hindu nationalist Bharatiya Janata Party (BJP) government of Delhi gave 390 acres of land and more than £160,000 for the setting up of gosadans or shelters for cows.

But all this apparent reverence and protection masks a trade in cows and cow products which involves unbelievable barbarity and cruelty.

Much of the abuse stems from the fact that the trade in and slaughter of cows is almost entirely clandestine and illegal - but the authorities which should be stopping it are routinely bribed to let it continue. There is, therefore, no scrutiny or regulation of the trade anywhere along the line.

Although Hindus hold the cow in special esteem, and Jains regard all life as so sacred that they try to avoid hurting insects, investigations show that all India's major communities are complicit in the cruel treatment of cows.

Hindu farmers allow their cows to be taken for slaughter. Muslims butcher them using primitive techniques in appalling conditions. Hindus, Jains, Sikhs, Muslims and Christians all profit.

And because much Indian beef finds its way to the Middle East and Europe from Kerala and Bangladesh - "we took up a lot of the slack from Britain caused by mad cow disease," says one authority - and leather products made from Indian cow hide are sold in High Street

They are so much ungrateful. They are taking milk from the cows, and when the milk is no more supplied, "All right, send it to the slaughterhouse." Once he has taken milk, he's indebted; again, it is being killed by him. So how much he has become entangled in his karma he does not know. Mudha. Duskrtino mudhah.
— Srila Prabhupada (Srimad-Bhagavatam 1.8.49, Mayapura, October 29, 1974)

shops such as Gap, the British consumer is also unknowingly benefiting from the abuse.

The slaughter of cows has been banned in all Indian states and territories except West Bengal, in the north-east, and Kerala in the far south. But there are hole-in-the-wall cow abattoirs dotted around the country, especially in Muslim quarters of towns and cities. But the main issue is an appalling traffic of cattle.

"There is a huge amount of trafficking of cattle to both West Bengal and Kerala," says Mrs Maneka Gandhi, former Minister of Social Justice and Empowerment in the government and a veteran campaigner against animal abuse of all sorts. "The ones going to West Bengal go by truck and train and they go by the millions. The law says you cannot transport more than 4 per truck but they are

putting in up to 70. When they go by train, each wagon is supposed to hold 80 to 100, but they cram in up to 900. I've seen 900 cows coming out of the wagon of a train, and 400 to 500 of them came out dead."

The trade exists because of gross corruption, Mrs Gandhi says. "An illegal organisation called the Howrah Cattle Association fakes permits saying the cattle are meant for agricultural purposes, for ploughing fields or for milk. The stationmaster at the point of embarkation gets 8,000 rupees per train-load for certifying that the cows are healthy and are going for milk.

"The government vets get X amount for certifying them as healthy. The cattle are unloaded just before Calcutta, at Howrah, then beaten and taken across to Bangladesh by road. Bangladesh, which has no cows of its own, is the biggest beef exporter in the region. Between 20,000 and 25,000 cows go across that border every day. You can make out the route taken by the trucks by the trail of blood they leave behind."

Even more horrifying is the transport of cows to the abattoirs on the border of Kerala in the extreme south of the peninsula. Mrs Gandhi says, "On the route to Kerala they don't bother with trucks or trains: they tie them and beat them and take them on foot, 20,000 to 30,000 per day." All Kerala's slaughter houses are on the border. "Because they have walked and walked and walked the cattle have lost a lot of weight, so to increase the weight and the amount of money they will receive, the traffickers make them drink water laced with copper sulphate, which destroys their kidneys and makes it impossible for them to pass the water - so when they are weighed they have 15kg of water inside them and are in extreme agony."

Ingrid Newkirk, President of Peta, followed one of the caravans of cattle stumbling towards Kerala. "It's a hideous journey," she writes in an issue of Animal Times, Peta's journal. "To keep them moving, drivers beat the animal across their hip bones, where there is no fat to cushion the blows. The cows are not allowed to rest or drink. Many cows sink to their knees. Drivers beat them and twist their battered tails to force them to rise. If that doesn't work they torment the cows into moving by rubbing hot chilli peppers and tobacco into their eyes."

When they finally make it to the slaughterhouses that stand on the Kerala border, the end they confront is unspeakable, Mrs Gandhi says.

In the age of Kali, the poor helpless animals, especially the cows, which are meant to receive all sorts of protection from the administrative heads, are killed without restriction. Thus the administrative heads under whose noses such things happen are representatives of God in name only. Such powerful administrators are rulers of the poor citizens by dress or office, but factually they are worthless, lower-class men without the cultural assets of the twice-born. No one can expect justice or equality of treatment from once-born (spiritually uncultured) lower-class men. Therefore in the age of Kali everyone is unhappy due to the maladministration of the state.

— Srila Prabhupada (Srimad Bhagavatam 1.17.5)

"In Kerala they also have a unique way of killing them - they beat their heads to a pulp with a dozen hammer blows. A well-intentioned visitor from the West, trying to improve slaughterhouse practice in Kerala, exhorted them to use stun guns, saying that the meat of an animal killed in this fashion (rather than having its throat slit) tasted sweeter. The stun guns that she left behind quickly broke and fell into disuse, but the belief that the meat was sweeter took hold - which explains this horrible method of slaughtering."

The sentimental attitude towards animals prevalent these days in the West is alien to traditional India, as to the rest of Asia. But respect and reverence for all life is fundamental to Hinduism - most Hindus are vegetarians even today - and the prevailing attitude is enshrined in

yas tvam krsne gate duram
saha-gandiva-dhanvana
socyo 'sy asocyan rahasi
praharan vadham arhasi
You rogue, do you dare beat an innocent cow because Lord Krsna and Arjuna, the carrier of the Gandiva bow, are out of sight? Since you are beating the innocent in a secluded place, you are considered a culprit and therefore deserve to be killed.

In a civilization where God is conspicuously banished, and there is no devotee warrior like Arjuna, the associates of the age of Kali take advantage of this lawless kingdom and arrange to kill innocent animals like the cow in secluded slaughterhouses. Such murderers of animals stand to be condemned to death by the order of a pious king like Maharaja Pariksit. For a pious king, the culprit who kills an animal in a secluded place is punishable by the death penalty, exactly like a murderer who kills an innocent child in a secluded place.

At least up to the time of Maharaja Pariksit, no one could imagine the wretched conditions of the cow and the bull. Maharaja Pariksit, therefore, was astonished to see such a horrible scene. He inquired whether the bull was not a demigod assuming such a wretched condition to indicate the future of the cow and the bull.
— *Srimad Bhagavatam (Srimad Bhagavatam 1.17.8)*

the Gandhian word ahimsa, "do no harm".

Yet greed, poverty, ignorance and absence of regulation and supervision have brought India's cows to the point where their treatment is on the threshold of becoming a major international scandal.

At root it is a political issue. The ban on cow slaughter has been a fundamental plank of the Hindu nationalists for many decades.

(By Peter Popham, The Independent, 14 February 2000)

19.

For The Crime of Taking A Walk

30 Cows Shot Dead In Full Public View

One fine morning, thirty cows from a farm in Wrexham in North Wales, UK, decided to take a walk. As they wandered into a housing estate, the police were called, and they managed to herd the cattle into a nearby field. An assessment was carried out by Wrexham Council, the police and the animal health and welfare authority, following which a decision was made to shoot the animals "for the protection of the public and the welfare of the animals". A council spokesperson said that the public were excluded from the area, but local parents claim that their children were traumatised after witnessing the slaughter "while out playing".

But these were simple cows, not African lions! Why was the decision made to shoot the cows in the field? Why where they not herded into a truck and taken back to the farm where they belonged? No regard for life whatsoever.

Council says cows may seem like benign, placid beasts, but they can be dangerous citing a case in 2009 where a vet was killed by a herd of cattle while out walking her dog.

It's also reported that the farmer who owned the cattle is facing court action, and as a consequence the council were unwilling to make any further comments.

Many people feel that the Council which led the decision to kill the animals, dealt with their escape very badly and believes the shooting should never have been carried out so close to Chirk Community School and Hospital in plain view of the patients and children.

John Pierce, the farmer says, "I have no civil words for the people who shot my animals. I've got two grandchildren at school in Chirk myself and the idea that any child should see such a thing makes me very angry. The poor youngsters who saw this must've been so traumatised. The need to shoot an animal is a very hard lesson to learn and for it to happen in this way is very sad."

Mr Pierce claims the animals were healthy and believes the decision to shoot them was made simply to avoid the inconvenience of having to deal with them if they escaped again.

He now has one cow left, a calf named Molly. Mr Pierce claimed he had to beg the council not to kill her and the only reason they spared her was because she had not escaped along with the rest of the herd.

He adds: "They didn't even tell me they were going to shoot the animals. The first I heard about it was when a friend called me up and told me."

Susan Elan Jones MP expressed her concerns about the incident. She says: "Several constituents have contacted me about the incident which caused considerable distress to those who witnessed it. I find it hard to understand why the cows could not have been rounded up and returned to their farms, instead of shot, especially in the full view of the public."

"I understand residents were given no advance warning of the shooting which happened in full view of patients in Chirk Community Hospital, who were naturally extremely shocked and upset. I am very keen to establish exactly what happened here."

This incident took place in March 2011. Around the same time in Swadlincote, another town of UK, a cow made a break for freedom while on its way to an abattoir, but was shot by firearms officers after it ended up in a graveyard.

It was a young cow, on her way to the abattoir in Swadlincote from the farm.. The farmer opened the door (of the transport vehicle) and it forced its way out through there.

They wouldn't come out through the other door as he opened the side and she got out. It was getting very distressed appeared to be wanting to escape by any means.

The cow fled managed to cover a quarter-of-a-mile to a church's graveyard before being confined.

Residents were surprised to see a cow because they are so used to see them in hamburgers.

One of the residents Mark Cooper says, "While I was on my way to work this morning an unusual sight was seen — a cow in Emmanuel Church's graveyard. Police were there but my first thoughts were how on earth did it get there and where had the cow come from."

They had firearms on the scene and the road around the church was shut off. Police left the scene at 10.30am, shortly after the animal was

Prabhupada: Now Kirtanananda was prosecuted because he is not killing cows.

Brahmananda: By having them grow old, they were saying that "This is cruelty. You should kill them."

Prabhupada: This is their civilization, that "You are not killing? You are cruel." Just see. Christ said, "Thou shall not kill." That is cruel. How can you pull on this civilization? But this is their religion. So what kind of persons they are?

—Srila Prabhupada (Room Conversation - February 28, 1977, Mayapur)

shot. A police spokesman said, "The cow needed dispatching, it had to be sent on its way."

Thus another cow's attempt at a great escape was foiled by the proud policemen.

Modern Life Is Founded On Disregard For Life and Nature

Modern life is characterized by a total lack of reverence towards life, both human and non-human.

In spite of the availability of so much food, billions of animals are mercilessly raised, transported and slaughtered every year. The reactions are equally severe for mankind. Human beings also get killed in riots, bombing and wars like the very animals they kill as a matter of fact.

A few birds when get infected with bird-flu, man starts killing millions of birds. Same thing happens when a few cows fall sick, they kill hundreds of thousands of cows. These things have no precedent in human history. This is cold blooded murder and holocaust. In God's kingdom, all beings have a right to live and one has to pay dearly for killing even an ant unnecessarily. Time is coming when people will 'cull' a whole race or nation when they get infected with a disease.

Perhaps this millennium has been the bloodiest of all human history. For about forty years after the discovery of the New World (America), it was legal to hunt down the natives like animals. It was only in 1530 that the Pope conceded that American Indians were human!

Mass killing has been a troubleshooting tool in the hands of World powers. Think of the Americans' plan for getting rid of almost everyone in North Vietnam. Shoot and bomb them until there are so few left

tatas canu-dinam dharmah
satyam saucam ksama daya
kalena balina rajan
nanksyaty ayur balam smrtih
Sukadeva Gosvami said: Then, O King, religion, truthfulness, cleanliness, tolerance, mercy, duration of life, physical strength and memory will all diminish day by day because of the powerful influence of the age of Kali.
~Srila Prabhupada (Srimad Bhagavatam 12.2.1)

that people think the problem has been solved. This philosophy was reflected in the attitude of Boris Yeltsin to the population of Chechnya. Same with Hitler's final solution for getting rid of the Jews and Stalin's final solution for getting rid of all small farmers in Russia. Same with the British in their colonies of Asia and Africa. Just kill and kill and kill! Whether its Afghanistan or Iraq, if you gonna solve a problem, just kill'em all. In Afghanistan, when Russian generals wanted to clear a minefield, they set the Russian infantry walking through it. They lost a lot of soldiers, but it certainly cleared the minefield.

No regard for life whatsoever. But the killers are unaware of the dire consequences awaiting them. Law of karma exacts more interest than any other bank in the world.

So without being devotee a man will become cruel, cruel, cruel, cruel, cruel, in this way go to hell. And devotee cannot tolerate. We have studied in the life of Lord Jesus Christ. When he saw that in the Jewish synagogue the birds were being killed, he became shocked. He therefore left. Jesus... He inaugurated the Christian religion. Perhaps you know. He was shocked by this animal-killing. And therefore his first commandment is "Thou shall not kill." But the foolish Christians, instead of following his instruction, they are opening daily slaughterhouses.
Srila Prabhupada (Srimad-Bhagavatam 7.9.52 — Vrndavana, April 7, 1976)

20.

The Funniest, Happiest Cow that Ever Lived

By Danielle Maestretti

Tucked away in a recent issue of Small Farmer's Journal, among discussions of sprouted horse feed and asparagus beetles, is Vermont farmer Suzanne Lupien's lovely remembrance of Nell, "the funniest, happiest cow that ever lived."

What a hard day to have to say goodbye to that gem of a cow I'd milked for 12 years, enjoying her marvelous personality as well as her creamy yellow milk. I hand-milk my six or eight cows, and have come

to value the time spent by their sides on the milk stool. Especially Nell! Her personality was so exuberant and fun, and so easy to read!

Nell was something of a rescue animal, as Lupien explains—injured, emaciated, a "little waif of a cow" when she joined Lupien's small farm—but she flourished, calved, produced wheel upon wheel of top-of-the-line camembert cheese, and lived to be 19. All with a great deal of personality, too,

Not only was she as fit as a fat fiddle, she was happy, and she never stopped expressing her enjoyment of and gratitude for all the good that came her way. Good hay! Apples and pumpkins! Rearing her own calf! Wonderful brushings! Fields and woods! Plus she had the cutest face and everyone loved her.

Open House potluck? She'd hone right in on the bowl of corn chips and suck them down before you could think of intercepting. Bread making in the outdoor oven? She knew when it was Friday and she'd sashay over to the bread table and inhale 20 lb. of bread dough and any warm loaves of bread stacked in baskets for the farmers market. Opportunities and ideas sprang up in her mind as fast as dandelions in a field.

You know how a cow behaves in spring finding herself in a lush green field for the first time? Twirling and jumping? She was the Ginger Rogers of the Fields. And when she was younger she didn't limit her performances to that initial turnout day—she did it anytime. It was impossible not to notice her exuberance, her glee: always coming when I called her, always ready for anything.

Goodbye, dear Nell. Thanks for being the best four-legged friend I've ever had! I've got three lovely cows to milk still, but it will never be the same without you.

Lupien's appreciation of her funny, spunky cow is quite beautiful, the sort of lively gem I love finding in Small Farmer's Journal, an oversized quarterly in which practical advice shares space with personal experiences like Lupien's.

21.

Yvonne - The World Famous Runaway Cow

Wrapped In A Mystery Inside A Forest

In Germany, a dairy cow named Yvonne's death-defying escape — and continued success in eluding capture — has become an incandescent symbol of freedom and animal dignity.

Now a popular subject on television and newspapers, Yvonne was being fattened up to be turned into steaks until she smashed through the electric fence of a farm in Aschau (Bavaria, Germany) and bounded off.

She escaped on May 24, 2011 and adopted a lifestyle that might be called Sherwoodian: sticking to forests, eluding police, and bringing acclaim and tourist dollars to her quaint village.

Curious visitors and search parties romped through the woods around Aschau, looking for signs of the cow.

Various bids to lure her back from the forest failed. They brought her calf and her best cow friend. They installed infrared cameras to find her.

Food traps were laid; a beagle hunting dog was enlisted. Other companion cows were sent in, to draw her out. But all to no avail.

Perhaps conceding the battle of wits - and the public-relations war - to the ruminant, officials hoped they can reach her through her heart. They brought in a male ox named Ernst, who they hoped would capture Yvonne's heart, and lure her back to human society.

Even a helicopter, equipped with a heat-seeking camera, was used.

She fled the helicopter and simply ignored what media dubbed the "George Clooney of cattle." Even Waltraud, Yvonne's sister, couldn't attract her out of the woods.

Yvonne was sold by an Austrian farmer to the farm in Aschau because she was nervous and jumpy. She was tethered for months, and her calf Friesi was taken away from her. Then one day she saw the other cows loading up to go off to the slaughterhouse, she decided that wasn't for her and she decided not to be turned into steak.

She Knew Exactly What She Was Doing

In fact, the case of a cow that eluded the best efforts of its pursuers has raised questions about the intellect lurking behind those bovine eyes. Did Yvonne really learn to outmanoeuvre humans? Was the beast the master of this cat and mouse game? Then again, how smart are the humans who would send a helicopter out after a cow?

"Yvonne knows exactly what she's doing, and she's tricking us," the manager of an animal rescue farm told a German newspaper.

Trackers who caught a glimpse of her claimed she had put on weight, which wasn't surprising given the smorgasbord of delicacies available to her in and around the woods - juicy grass, ample supplies of apples and maize.

Once, in the dead of night, one intrepid tracker crept into the woods

to stalk her. She appeared out of the mist, and stared him straight in the eyes. She walked off before he could fire a dart at her.

With every failed attempt to capture her, Yvonne's fame grew, as did her ability to outsmart her pursuers. She wised up to the sound of rotor blades, car doors, walkie-talkies and mobile phones, dashing into the undergrowth as soon as she heard them.

Government pursuers complained that she had even grown accustomed to their shift rota, always staying out of sight in the afternoons when they had finished their lunch, and venturing out just before dawn when they were asleep.

One expert tracker was so determined to get her that he crept through the woods in his socks to avoid making a sound, but it was to no avail.

The World media portrayed Yvonne to be a kind of freedom fighter for the animals kingdom. This was a cow who refused to be cowed down. The media devoted as much attention to Yvonne's exploits as they did to the euro debt crisis, nuclear energy policy and unrest in the Middle-East. Millions were transfixed and followed daily reports about her sightings. Her blog recorded thousands of hourly hits.

Telepathy Contact

Franziska Matti, an animal communication expert from Berne in Switzerland, said she had managed to contact Yvonne using telepathy. "I spoke to her yesterday and she said that she was fine but didn't feel ready to come out of hiding," said Matti.

"She said she knew that Ernst had been waiting for her but that she was scared. She said she thought that humans would lock her up and she would no longer be free."

Shooting Orders

After she nearly collided with a police car, local authorities put a bounty on her head with a shoot-to-kill order, calling her "a public danger" and a "traffic hazard".

Of all the animals, man is the only one that is cruel. He is the only one that inflicts pain for the pleasure of doing it.
—Mark Twain

71

But an international hue and cry soon followed, forcing the district authority to revoke the orders.

The authority said in a statement, "As the animal no longer constitutes an acute threat to road traffic in its current location, no major search or capture operations are necessary. The Mühldorf district office requests that the animal not be disturbed in its current habitat."

Yvonne finally had won her freedom, and could now roam to her heart's content through the Bavarian forest where she has found refuge.

This was the news Yvonne's army of fans had been waiting for. A Facebook page set up in her honor had over 27,000 friends, and media from around the world devoted copious column inches to her adventures, possibly in a bid to feature some light relief from the Libyan war and financial market turmoil. Her celebrity status evidently helped to protect her.

Bild, the tabloid German newspaper, offered •10,000 ($14,500) for information leading to her safe capture, and provided almost daily coverage of the hunt, even paying a vet to examine one of her cowpats. He declared she was healthy and well-fed.

Hindus of The World Come Out In Support

Prominent Hindus, for whom cows are sacred, weighed in with calls on German authorities to protect Yvonne.

Hindu statesman Rajan Zed, in a statement in Nevada (USA) argued that decision of the authorities giving permission to shoot her was "ill advised" and should be immediately withdrawn.

Zed, who is President of Universal Society of Hinduism, applauded the efforts of animal rights groups to save her. Hindus would gladly adopt "Yvonne", Zed stressed.

> *When these people take these cows to the slaughterhouse, animal stockyard, they understand. Very recently, about few years ago, some..., that animal stock store was some way or other broken and all the cows began to... Perhaps you know. It was published in the... And they were shot down. Shot to death. They were fleeing like anything, that "We shall save ourselves."*
>
> *—Srila Prabhupada (Srimad-Bhagavatam 1.10.4 — Mayapura, June 19, 1973)*

Rajan Zed pointed out: Cow is worshipped by Hindus world over. Rig-Veda, the oldest existing scripture of the mankind, describes cow as aghnya (not slayable). Lord Krishna, shown as cowherd many times, is also known as Gopala (protector of cows). There is a belief that cow was created the same day as Brahma (creator god). Also referred as "Mother Cow", this divine animal, venerated from an early period, is the abode of many deities in Hinduism. Mahatma Gandhi reportedly said, "I yield to none in my worship of the cow".

Until The Cow Comes Home

In the end, undone by loneliness, Yvonne turned herself in, wandering near a farm in the town of Muhldorf and trying to engage the other cows grazing there. She apparently got tired of being lonely, after three months on the run.

Konrad Gutmann, 46, claimed the •10,000 reward offered by the German tabloid Bild after the seemingly lonely animal wandered into his meadows to befriend his cows. "It was just luck really. I was out taking a tour of my electric fence with my daughter Melanie at about 6pm when I saw Yvonne on the other side staring at the young cows.

"She seemed lonely," Gutmann told the Daily Mail. "She went back into the woods when she saw us. I got up behind her and my daughter gathered the cows in one area of the field." The cow was finally herded into the field. "She was very nervous,' added the farmer. "You could see the stress of the past days and weeks had taken its toll on her."

The Gut Aiderbichl animal sanctuary promptly moved Yvonne to her new home. They were able to confirm her identify by the tag on her ear.

In keeping with the bullish nature that had preserved her freedom until now, Yvonne did not go quietly. Pictures reveal she put up a

Cruelty to dumb animals is one of the distinguishing vices of low and base minds. Wherever it is found, it is a certain mark of ignorance and meanness; a mark which all the external advantages of wealth, splendour, and nobility, cannot obliterate. It is consistent neither with learning nor true civility.
—William Jones

significant fight before being tranquillised on and transported to the sanctuary.

It was a dramatic end to a story that gripped the World for much of the summer in 2011.

Cyn Valentine

Bright Future Beckons

Yvonne's fate became internationally known because she made a clear statement: 'I am an animal, I can live in the forest, and I don't want to have anything to do with humans because they have treated me badly.'

Wildlife charity Gut Aiderbichl, which purchased Yvonne, said in a statement, "Yvonne truly fought for her freedom. She shown the world that the urge to be free is strong — even for a cow."

Michael Aufhauser, the founder of the charity said, "Yvonne's odyssey has finally drawn attention to the plight of cows. People tend to ignore cattle even though they are such important animals for us. Now they are talking about the conditions in which cattle are kept, transported and slaughtered."

Yvonne's transformation from an ordinary, if unhappy, dairy cow into an increasingly shaggy wild beast also revealed that cows still retain the powerful survival instincts in spite of their long domestication. This also shows that, deep down, cows have a fire in their four bellies for freedom just like humans.

For Yvonne now a bright future beckons. She has been taken to a sanctuary that describes itself as "positively Indian" in its respect for animals. There, she will be able to live out her days grazing peacefully alongside her son Friesi and her sister Waltraud, who have also been purchased by the sanctuary.

A Cow Humanised

Yvonne was a run-of-the-mill farm cow but reporting on this runaway cow humanised her. Not only was "who" used to refer to it, but "she" and "her" as well.

In another sense she was not "a run-of-the-mill farm cow." To begin with, she has a human name, Yvonne, and a sister with the name Waltraut. There is also a bull named Ernst and she has a son too. Who wouldn't be tempted to humanise this story? Yvonne also seems to be

Anybody for some Yvonne burgers? I didn't think so. Why is it we feel uncomfortable eating an animal with a name, when all of the nameless others like her have just as much personality and will to live? — Roger Perrone

unusually spirited.

What the public found chilling in the story was how hunters were encouraged to shoot Yvonne on sight, with a promise of a huge reward, and how a lot of people were driven by greed to try to catch the poor cow.

As it happened, Germans only now realise that there is something special about the bovine known affectionately as Yvonne, which has since captured the hearts of a nation.

Better late than steaks, some might say.

I have seen in New Vrindaban. One cow, she was crying because her calf was taken away. So she was feeling so sorry. Now in our New Vrindaban, we see how the cows are happy, how they are dealing. They are not afraid. This is our duty, to keep the cows happy. Just like I want to see my wife and children happy, similarly, it is the duty of the human society to see that the cows feeling very happy. This is human civilization. Otherwise it is tiger civilization, meat-eaters. Meat is not eaten by human being. It is eaten by the dogs, by the tigers, by the animals.

So we have created a society for killing cows and eating the meat and maintaining slaughterhouse in the name of religion. This is going on. So how we can be happy? There cannot be happiness. It is not a sentiment. Therefore this is most sinful activity, meat-eating, cow killing. Most sinful activity. And you have to suffer for that. Unfortunately, these rascals, they do not know that what is the result of this sinful activity. They think the life will go on, and there is no more life. "After finishing of this body, everything will be finished." Atheistic theory. Bhasmi-bhutasya dehasya kutah punar agamano bhavet. Kutah. "Oh, who is coming?" But that they do not know, rascals. We get information from Krsna, tatha dehantara-praptih: "Oh, you have to accept another body after finishing this body." But they are not responsible. They are so irresponsible, they do not care for the next life, the result of pious and sinful activities.

— Srila Prabhupada (Lecture, Srimad-Bhagavatam 1.10.4, London, November 25, 1973)

22.
Until The Cows Come Home

Cows are notoriously languid creatures and make their way home at their own unhurried pace. That's certainly the imagery behind the phrase 'till the cows come home' or 'until the cows come home' which means 'for a long but indefinite time.'

The precise time and place of the coining of this colloquial phrase isn't known. It was certainly before 1829 though, and may well have been in Scotland. The phrase appeared in print in The Times in January that year, when the paper reported a suggestion of what the Duke of Wellington should do if he wanted to maintain a place as a minister in Peel's cabinet:

"If the Duke will but do what he unquestionably can do, and propose a Catholic Bill with securities, he may be Minister, as they say in Scotland - until the cows come home."

23.

"Help! My Cow Speaks Cantonese!"

China's most ambitious projects of the last two decades, the Three Gorges Dam and the South-North Water Diversion, have required hundreds of thousands of villagers to move to new homes far from where they were born.

For the residents of Xingang village in Guangdong province, it's ten years since the government moved them from their birthplace in Chongqing Municipality, to an area 1,500 kilometers from their original homes.

Integration into their new hometown is a long process and will take a lot longer than ten years.

At first, lots of migrants couldn't get used to life in Guangdong and wanted to return to Chongqing.

Most of the migrants didn't have that option – they had nothing left in their home region; relatives and friends had also been relocated.

Migrants have encountered many difficulties, one of the biggest being the language— it's hard for them to learn Cantonese, the Guangdong dialect.

Local people can always tell that they are migrants by their accent.

Still they are able to manage the language issue with the locals somehow. But the toughest part is dealing with the animals!

After buying a cow in Guangdong, one migrant says that he couldn't get the animal to obey him. It was used to Cantonese, and didn't understand the Chongqing dialect of its new master!

"Human society needs only sufficient grain and sufficient cows to solve its economic problems. All other things but these two are artificial necessities created by man to kill his valuable life at the human level and waste his time in things which are not needed."
—*Srila Prabhupada (Srimad Bhagavatam 3.2.29)*

24.

Reuniting Mother And Baby

By Ellie Laks

While we were rescuing this years Thanksgiving turkey at a local ranch, we couldn't help but notice the horrific conditions in which the other animals were living. Unable to stomach what we were witnessing, we came home with two of the ten cows who were in the worst shape and were pregnant.

When they got home to The Gentle Barn, one of the cows seemed inconsolably distraught. She was trying to get out of the pen, pacing, sweating, and mooing as though screaming for someone. Throughout

the first night, she kept crying out, barely pausing to take a breath.

At first, we thought her stress was from missing all of the animals she had left behind, or from feeling unsure of her new surroundings. But by morning, when her cries had not stopped, we realized something more serious was going on. We also noticed that her udder was full now and she was expressing milk. When we called back to the place we rescued her from, our fears were confirmed. She had been separated from her calf, and we were informed that her baby was being sold that day to someone else for slaughter. We demanded that they release the baby to us, knowing that this cow would die of heartbreak otherwise, and they agreed, especially because their truck had broken down and they couldn't deliver the calf to the other people and we had a trailer...small miracles!

When we arrived at The Gentle Barn with the calf, his mom heard his voice, she jumped up and practically broke through the pasture fencing to get to her calf. When we lead her tiny baby to reunite with her, the calf collapsed on the ground in front of her. As she licked him and nuzzled him with the gentlest touch, he got up. As her baby nursed, for the first time in twelve hours, the mom let out a long moo, like the biggest sigh of relief. Now that her baby is with her, she has not made a single sound. She is happy and at peace, and the two will never be separated again.

The offending ranch has been sighted and is in the process of being shut down, but there are still seven cows there that we are desperately trying to get out, before they are slaughtered. There are two pregnant cows, one with a calf, and four calves that have been weaned.

(The Gentle Barn was founded by Ellie Laks in 1999 in Santa Clarita, CA. The Gentle Barn is currently home to 130 animals who are rescued from severe abuse, neglect or slaughter. Once the animals are rehabilitated they stay at the barn for the rest of their lives and serve as ambassadors helping to heal abused children. The Gentle Barn is host to kids in foster care, on probation, in gangs, on drugs and from the inner city, as well as school groups and special needs kids and adults. Through the interactions with the animals and their stories, kids learn kindness, compassion, confidence and reverence for all life.)

25.

Cow That Helped World War II Prisoners Escape

Kachadore Berberian, owner of Berberian Farm in Northborough, USA, recalls his incredible journey out of war.

A cow turned out to be the lucky token by which he and two other men hinged an escape from a German prisoner camp during WWII.

He's a farmer in real life, but in Germany, 1945, Kachadore "Kachie" Berberian pretended to be one to escape prison and slip out of enemy territory.

It was 1945, the war neared its end, and the Germans were close to surrender. But Berberian, weak and starving, got out amidst the bombing of the city of Dresden. The journey depicts winding, aimless months of scrounging, bartering, walking, ingenuity and luck that surely brought Berberian closer to death than he ever knew.

Berberian, a well-known and likable character in Northborough as the longtime owner of Berberian Farms, says he rarely shares the tale of his wartime trial.

At 87, with a gravelly voice and animated arms, he recounts the steps to freedom with remarkable accuracy and vividness.

The middle of three Berberian boys, the U.S. Army drafted him in March of 1944, and after weeks of training in Florida and Indiana, he was stationed in England. Thirty days in England brought him down the English Channel to the front lines in France, and then to Belgium, where the Battle of the Bulge had just started. In the dense, vast Ardennes Forest in Germany, Berberian was surrounded by mayhem and uncertainty in the darkness.

"On Dec. 16 of 1944, the Bulge started," said Berberian, "and in my division, within three days we lost half the division. That's how bad it was. My regiment was surrendered, what was left of it, to the Germans. I had only spent 16 days on the line, and three in actual battle."

The next six months, he said, "was worse than being in combat."

For 30 days, Berberian was in a concentration camp with American and British soldiers. Every day, he was granted a tin cup with turnip skins, salt and pepper, for his one meal. Two men were assigned to each cot, so they had to take turns sleeping. After the 30 days, the Germans gathered groups of 60 men together for "working commandos," and they were all shipped to Dresden.

Crammed into tiny boxcars, they sat and slept upright, elbows curled to their sides, and used their helmets as bathroom facilities. It took a week to get to Dresden. One interaction in that dark boxcar sticks in Berberian's mind to this day.

"It was Christmas Eve day," he said. "It was at night and the train was moving and you could hear one guy crying and he said to somebody, 'If I only had a cigarette.' By chance, I managed to save a few cigarettes. I took one out and passed it down to the guy. He said that was the best Christmas present he ever got. You could buy your life through a cigarette. I wouldn't even recognize the guy. I couldn't see. But that stuck with me."

Getting in to Dresden, the third largest city in Germany, the mood was bleak, and the city sat in ruins. Between 100,000 and 150,000 civilians had been killed, and buildings were demolished, bombed by the British.

Berberian was crammed in to the room with the other 59 men. There were no showers, or hot water, but there were toilets, and running water. Here, they were given a pound of potatoes per man per day. Steal another man's potatoes, and the other 59 could each take a swing, by their own rules. It happened, once, when Berberian was there, and he said, "you couldn't recognize the guy when they got done."

Up at 5 a.m., Berberian walked with the others four miles to a furniture factory to work by 7 a.m. In the dead of winter, it was below—far below—freezing, so no one dreamed of dashing off from the one old guard with the rifle.

"You never got any news," said Berberian, "and there are always rumors, but they're never true. We worked about four and a half months that way."

Word that the Russians were coming sent the commando and lots of others to be moved to another town, up a mountain that was about 1,000 feet above sea level. Around April, when the "Russians are coming" was more imminent, everyone was thrown to the streets. Not knowing where they were going, they were marched by guards through roads loaded with other POWs, civilians and military.

"About a half a day went by and guys are falling down weak, including myself," said Berberian. "We were having a hard time just going to the bathroom. That's how weak a lot of guys got. They were marching us and we had very few guards doing this. We came along this truck that had been bombed and it was loaded with vodka, and everybody got crazy grabbing bottles."

With two bottles of vodka cradled under his armpits, Berberian was confronted by a German soldier, who demanded the booze. The soldier was drunk, and Berberian wouldn't let go.

"I said to him, 'flesh! flesh! flesh!" said Berberian. "Now flesh is meat in German. And he lets go of the tug of war and off he goes. And 20 minutes goes by and the next thing you know he comes out with a live cow. I give him the booze, he gives me the cow. I thought, the 60 of us are going to be able to eat meat for the first time.

"Now I've got this cow, and it's about three in the afternoon and I've had it. I don't have the energy to hang on to this cow anymore. It's in the gutter, it's here, it's there, it's everywhere. So I said to these two other guys, 'Look, you grab his tail and the other his ear and we'll walk off with this cow as a group. We're going to drop dead anyway, so let's take our chances.' We walked and walked and no one said nothing to us. They must have thought we were a couple of farmers that were just going."

With the cow between them, the three ran into a German farmer, who gave them something to eat. He and his wife were packing to flee, too. Walking toward freedom was becoming easier, and hanging on to the cow was not; he handed the cow over to the farmer.

The three kept going, to Czechoslovakia. Berberian lost 50 pounds during the journey.

Germany in turmoil, they got food where they could. Once, a German captain demanded that one of his soldiers hand over some bread and cheese. Sometimes, the three would split up and search for food. Other times, they'd enter abandoned homes, or knock on a door and ask for a bed and a meal. A woman carrying a one-year-old child talked her way into being part of the traveling crew for a while.

"She took that kid and throws it on her shoulder," said Berberian. "We walked until 2 in the morning. I just couldn't walk no more. I had cramps in my crotch and couldn't do it. She saw a house and walked to it, but they gave her a bad time. But they allowed us in. I woke up the next morning and I couldn't walk. We stayed there for three days, and there were six Russian prisoners that were with us that were really bold. They insisted we have dinner with them, and let me tell you, they were wild. They wanted women and everything else. We just wanted to get out, stay alive and be liberated."

Ultimately, the trio ditched the woman (as well as another who was in their company for a while), and ran into some Russians with a broken truck. Berberian told 'em how to fix it, so they gave him a ride—a ride to Prague, where they were finally free.

"We were free, really, from the day we got that cow," said Berberian. "But we stayed in Prague for three weeks, and slept in a vacant building in the hallway. After three weeks, we were awoken in the morning by an American captain and I said, 'How the hell did you find us?' The Russians had told him."

An ambulance transported them to a hospital camp in Czechoslovakia, where Berberian was too "healthy" to get a cot, and had to make room for the sickest. When the names came out every morning, Berberian looked. He was to be at a certain point on the field at 9 a.m. He was and a DC3 plane was there, transporting him to Reims, France, where he regained his strength, and was transported to the U.S. to fully recover.

The first thing he asked for when he got back? Not a steak. A whopping ice cream cone.

(By Charlene Arsenault)

"*What is wrong in wanting to stop killing of an animal from which man benefits the most. Most people wouldn't eat a dog as its man's best friend. Then why eat cows, whose milk every human baby is weaned on ? Hindus Love cows for a reason, we owe them a debt.*"
—*Misha, India*

26.

Humble Ox

Playing His Role Since Time Immemorial

To say that the humble "ox" played a pivotal role in European history might to some appear rather strange, but to the people of Salzberg, Austria, this beast is a symbol of courage in the face of adversity.

In the 1500s, an enemy army laid a seize to the city of Salzburg, depriving the inhabitants of food and drink. Their cupboards bare with

nary a bit of food left, the people were practically ready to surrender until they found a lone ox roaming the streets. They paraded the beast in front of the invaders to prove that they were not hungry.

Then, during the night, they painted it black to show the next day that they had more than enough food for the people to survive as testified by another living bull. Completely confused, the army retreated, leaving the people of Salzberg in peace. People were lucky to find an alive bull. Probably a living bull is worth much more than a dead one!

Beneath the placid, easy-going and unpretentious exterior of the ox lies a kind heart, a modest amount of ambition, and a willingness to bear heavy burdens that might overwhelm others, not to mention a strong sense of loyalty. This is a revered animal who symbolizes diligence, reliability, sincerity, strength and sound judgment. But don't expect these lumbering souls to have a sparkling sense of humor or be at all style conscious.

For centuries and millenniums, ox has been used for plowing, logging, parades, religious ceremonies, sports (in pulling or driving contests), general farm work or simply as a pack animal (an animal that carries cargo on its back).

27.

A Day With Krishna's Cows In Vraja

By Parsada dasi

During kartik last year, a very dear friend of mine, Padma visited Sri Vrindavan Dham, and a sincere devotee for many years. She arrived a day after the much celebrated Gopastami festival. As we made our way to the ISKCON goshala that afternoon, I described to her our Gopastami festival, where Srimati Radharani is dressed as the cowherd boy Subal and at this time Her devotees relish the sweet darshan of Her lotus feet, the only time in the year except Radhastami. On this wonderful day also Their Lordships Krsna and Balaram visit Their cows

at the goshala, riding on a palanquin lead by the vibrant chanting and dancing of the devotees. You can't help but notice Their appreciative smiles as They examine Their calves, bulls and cows.

The whole day devotees are plunged into an ecstasy of dramas, lectures, exotic prasadam and go-seva. She was really sorry for having missed the festival. I asked her what she thought about the Supreme Personality of Godhead appearing as a cowherd boy in Vraja. "Come to think about it, it never struck me as something important, I just took it for granted, you know, it's in all of Srila Prabhupada's lectures, books and purports. Its there, and something I accepted without much thought."

What she said next shocked me. "What to speak of realizing Krsna as a cowherd boy, I have never touched a cow in my life! I have been to Vrindavan a few times but between my kids, the husband, their getting sick, the morning program, parikramas, loi bazaar and the MVT restaurant, there was no time for the cows. We often saw the stray cows but my kids were too scared to go anywhere near them. I know I should have spared some time to visit the goshala, for them to get used to the cows but we never had enough time. Today will be my first visit and without my family, I should feel guilty but somehow don't. My mom is

As soon as Krsna and Balarama were a little grown up, They were meant for taking care of the calves. Although born of a very well-to-do family, They still had to take care of the calves. This was the system of education. Those who were not born in brhmana families were not meant for academic education. The brahmanas were trained in a literary, academic education, the ksatriyas were trained to take care of the state, and the vaisyas learned how to cultivate the land and take care of the cows and calves. There was no need to waste time going to school to be falsely educated and later increase the numbers of the unemployed. Krsna and Balarama taught us by Their personal behavior. Krsna took care of the cows and played His flute, and Balarama took care of agricultural activities with a plow in His hand.
— Srila Prabhupada (Srimad Bhagavatam 10.11.37)

taking good care of them. Thank you very much for bringing me." she said.

"Its only fair then that I should introduce you to the bliss of serving Krsna's cows and have an inkling of why the Supreme Personality of Godhead appeared as a cowherd boy." "I am the humble servant of Krsna's cows, please lead the way!" she said laughingly.

As we entered our ISKCON goshala, the smell of cow dung, cow urine and freshly copped grass filled the air. A few cowherd women were busy picking up cow-dung in a metal pan; a few young boys were washing the cowsheds with buckets of water and elsewhere the cowherd men were leading the bulls out of the sheds into the sunshine. Over the loudspeakers, Prabhupada's sweet bhajans played in the background. I watched the happy look on my friends face and gave her, her first assignment, "Please take that pan from this mataji and you go to that part of the barn and fill it up with cow-dung."

With an amazed look her face, she turned to me, "You can't be serious!" she said. After giving her a practical demonstration, she went down on her knees and picked up her first handful of cowdung. And in no time she had the pan filled up. She was having so much fun; she then carried it on her head and took it to the area where it would be

made into cow-dung cakes. Sitting among the ladies who were already making them, she made over a dozen cowdung cakes!

Next we got buckets and filled them with fresh sweet water and she carried them to every cow in the shed, it was tiring for she is not one to do menial labor. "Keeping a maid has made me lazy", she quipped as she placed the bucket next to Jamuna a beautiful white cow who gave birth a week ago, her udders full, Jamuna drank up all the water and mooed for more.

Giving her back a massage, she panted, "Could I take a break now?" "Sure" I replied. We went over to where the baby calves were kept, there were about five of them sitting huddled together enjoying the sunshine. That did it, she crouched down picked up Jamuna's baby, placed him on her lap and began caressing and kissing him. Every time he jolted back, she held him tighter. "You are sooooooooo beautiful, eh, sooooooooo beautiful!" And beautiful he was, white as snow except for his forehead and the tip of his tail, which had a sprinkling of brown. She looked at me, "He is mine! I want to take him home, my boys will love him."

"Of course you can take him home, in your heart, and photos should suffice for your boys, till you bring them to Vrindavan." I said. "Can't believe the fun I am having, it's like another world."

"It is another world," I said. After much hesitation she put the calf down. "Give him a name" I said. She looked up at me surprised, "Gosh! I can name him too! ok, I will call him Jamuna Priya, I will never forget him."

"Alright, its time to feed the cows laddus," I said. "Oh! Wonderful! Let's get those laddus." After we got a basket full of laddus, she wanted to know what they were made of, "jaggery and coarse wheat," I said. "They smell yummy, are they good for human consumption?" she asked jokingly.

She went around feeding the cows and big calves laddus and at one time she let out a scream, "They have teeth! One just bit me!" I examined her fingers, "You got the mercy, and I said, millions of your sinful activities have been destroyed, you will be ok." "Oh, really, and how does that work?" she questioned. "You see, the 33 million demigods live in the body of these cows, especially these ones with the silky soft skin folds at the neck, lotus eyes and the huge hump on the back. Also residing in their bodies are the nine planets. Remember that time when you sent me an email saying me that your husband was in his Saturn period?"

"Yes, I never knew this, so instead of doing this and all the other things, my mother-in-law insisted I do the Shiva puja, Durga puja and read the Hanuman Chalisa, we could have just worshipped Go-mata, why didn't you tell me?"

"At that time I was also not aware of the importance of worshipping Krsna's cows. Its only by their causeless mercy, I can render some service to them. Its getting closer to milking time, we have a few minutes left, lets go brush Luxman, my favorite bull, he sometimes bring Krsna Balaram's milk to the temple." I said.

We went over to Luxman lying with the other bulls under the pipal trees, as soon as he saw us he got up and held up his head high, a huge copper red bull. I pulled out from my bag a special brush, with firm bristles to brush Luxman. "Krishna! He is such a big bull, you sure he will not toss me back to my hellish country," she retorted staying a little distance away. "Not at all, he is the gentlest and sweetest of all the bulls

in the goshala," I said as I began brushing Luxman under the neck, on his back, the hump, between his horns, his head. He loved it. Seeing how much he was enjoying the brushing, my friend grabbed the brush from my hands saying, "Come on, give me the brush, you are too slow, Luxman wants a full body brush, I am expert in these things, having a husband and two sons, you know!!"

I laughed as she got into the swing of brushing Luxman, he loved it so much so, that he practically fell asleep while standing up and after some time he sat done and dozed off, not before she put a couple of laddus in his enormous mouth.

Hugging me as we went to the milking pen, my friend with tears in her eyes said, "Thank you, I never knew cows can be such lovable, sweet and gentle animals, no wonder Krsna loved them so much, I cannot in my wildest dreams ever think, I would ever feel so much happiness and closer to Krsna."

"It's not over yet, you have to milk at least one cow and then we will together relish the chanting of the Lords holy name amongst the cows," I said.

As we entered the milking pen, the cowherd men had the milking cows back legs tied with ropes and into a silver pail fell thick, creamy white milk as they gently pressed the udders between their thumbs and forefingers. Continuous streams of frothy milk rapidly started filling the pails.

My friend could contain herself no longer; she squatted besides Shyam the cowherd boy. He gave her a crimson smile and taught her how to milk Kalindi, at first Kalindi protested, after repeated attempts my friend finally milked her first cow! It was a historical moment. She was jubilant; she danced, gave me repeated hugs, kissed Kalindi and hugged Shyam as well!

Just see Krsna's picture, how He's loving the cow. You see? He is instructing by His practical life how He is compassionate with the cows.

Krsna is habituated to take care of the cows. Just like nowadays any respectable gentleman is supposed to take care of dog
— Srila Prabhupada (Lecture, Jakarta, February 27, 1973)

As the milking went on, we sat under the kadamba tree, surrounded by Krsna's beloved cows and with our minds fixed on the Lords holy name, chanted five rounds. "This is the best japa, I ever did, and everything seems so mystical and pure. It seems as if I am in another time zone, actually it seems as if I am closer to Krsna, a truly unbelievable experience, something to relish, cherish and keep locked away in the heart.

We lead such hectic lives, twenty four seven, its about work, money, keeping house, seeing to the kids and pleasing the in-laws. My husband is busy with his job and we hardly see him. I make it to the temple on Sunday's but its not enough, I want to do more, what can I do, please tell me what I can do for the cows," she said looking at me. I smiled, gave her a hug and told her to share her experience with others. Just as the holy name is non-different from Krsna, He can never be separated from His beloved cows in Vraja. "Also promote go-seva amongst your friends and family members and support this project according to your means." "I will" she said. As we made our way back to the temple she picked up a dried cow-dung patty and put it in her bag, looking at me, she said, "for memories and purifying my home and heart."

28.

A Good Life Makes For Happy Cows

At Hare Krishna farm

By Julie Jammot

Milked by hand, allowed to breed naturally and free from the threat of slaughter, the cows at Gokul farm near London could be possibly the happiest in Britain.

The 44 animals are owned by a community of Hare Krishnas, who live on the site at Aldenham bequeathed by Beatles guitarist George Harrison.

As believers of a branch of Hinduism, the Hare Krishnas view cows as sacred and treat them with respect, milking them by hand for the animals' comfort and allowing them to calve less intensively than in industrial farms.

Crucially, the community members are also vegetarian, guaranteeing that the cows are at no risk of slaughter.

"They are very sensitive animals. It's like if you have a dog — how you feel, the dog senses that," says Shyamasundara Das, the head of the farm at Aldenham.

"Here, because we have an

atmosphere of cow care, the animals themselves are a lot more peaceful and tranquil, and maybe it's also because there is no sense that they are going to be killed by us."

There are occasional massages, careful milking twice a day, and the spacious living quarters — the community has recently installed new cowsheds in French oak — the farm may well be the bovine equivalent of a five-star hotel.

The cattle pay their way by pulling carts to take groups of school children or young families around the farm, as well as powering a traditional mill to grind the cereal that feeds the cows.

The farm is built next to the Bhaktivedanta Manor, which Harrison donated to the Hare Krishna movement in the early 1970s and is now their British base.

The presence of the sacred cows adds a spiritual element and brings the community closer to the Hindu ideal of a simple life in harmony with nature.

"Krishna is always seen surrounded by cows. He was a cow herd boy 5,000 years ago in India," says Kripamoya Das, a Hare Krishna priest.

There is also a more practical link between the believers and the cows.

The flowers used to decorate Deities in the temple next to the manor, where barefoot believers pray morning, noon and night, are fed to the cows once they begin to droop, as a thank you for all their hard work.

Although their humane approach means that calves are allowed to continue suckling their mothers' milk for far longer than in industrial farms, the cows at Gokul still produce a large amount of milk.

At the moment this is drunk only by the community at Aldenham, but Shyamasundara Das is keen to begin selling it the world outside.

However, the cost

of such a feel-good product is a barrier. The milk currently costs about three pounds (3.5 euros, 4.7 dollars) a litre and, pending the approval of regulators, would be sold at a hefty 3.5 pounds a litre, making it perhaps the most expensive cow's milk in Europe.

And is it any better than normal milk?

Mark Gardener, a vet who regularly visits Gokul farm, feels so. He is confident that the cows here are likely to be happier.

"Normally in a dairy farm each cow has to justify his position" by having calves every few months or producing sufficient milk, and if they don't they will be sent to slaughter, he says.

"Whereas here the cows aren't under that pressure."

Interesting Facts About Cows

Cows have been known to walk for miles to find their calves.

Cows like to sleep close to their families

Sleeping arrangements are determined by their position in the social hierarchy.

There are approximately 920 different breeds of cows in the world.

Cows have incredible senses: they have near panoramic vision, can detect odours up to five miles away and they can hear low and high frequency sounds better than humans.

29.

When Friends Just Stand By

Waiting For The Inevitable

By Lewis Donohew

A cow was down in the front pasture. I saw her for the first time
as I walked out to the mailbox to pick up the morning newspaper.
The cow was lying near the pond, the front of her sitting up and her
back legs stretched out behind her. When I approached her, she tried to
crawl forward with her front legs but her back legs wouldn't cooperate.
Her big brown eyes looked at me and she made a low sound, half

moo, half moan.

Grazing nearby were two other cows, like friends attending the sick. They weren't used to much human contact and spent their days roaming the pastures, feeding on the lush grasses. Only in winter when they were fed silage from the silo did they have some contact with humans and that was only slight. All the workman did was push a button to start the silo unloader and the auger that spread feed along a trough. Ordinarily they would have been skittish. Yet here they were looking at me with what I thought was considerable trust and some expectation, as if they felt I could help their friend.

I called my cattle partner, who came over and tried to roll the cow over, but it was obvious she couldn't get up. Other cows, noticing us there, came to watch. I wondered if the cow's back had been injured, maybe by the bull trying to mount her, or if she was suffering from some ailment. At that moment, as if in response to my thought, the bull meandered over and stood staring at me. He was a sturdy young fellow, a red-haired Limousin, and easily could have done the damage. He was neither gentle nor malicious. He didn't chase people or cows, but he went where he wanted to when he wanted to and one needed to stay out of his way. At the moment, he merely wanted to watch and I didn't need to move.

It was hard to judge the cow's age. I asked my cattle partner what we should do. He said the cow was old and almost toothless but he didn't know what was wrong with her either and he didn't know of anything we could do right now but water her.

"If she don't get back up soon, I'll call the vet," he said.

When the vet got there, he said the same things we had concluded. She either was injured by a bull trying to mount her or something went out in her back. She is getting some age on her, he added.

"I'd say in cow years, she's about sixty. She may have just worn out." He stood up from his kneeling position beside the cow. "I can put her down if you want me to."

"What are the alternatives?" I asked.

"There aren't many. You could put some feed out by her and give her some water. Pour some of it over her to cool her off now and then. If she doesn't get up on her own soon, she's not going to make it."

The next day, she was lying down. She still raised her head when I came over but her stomach had swollen and she obviously wasn't doing well. Through it all, the two cows were keeping vigil. My partner had left feed and water for her, but today she had taken nothing. On the following day, she was dead. We called the dead wagon, the people who come and remove dead animals. This time the bull was nowhere in sight.

I guess that's the way it is when you get old. One day you fall and break a hip or you get sick and a few good friends come and sit with you during your final days. The doctor looks at you like a piece of meat and maybe does something to ease your pain and then they wait for you to die. Then the dead wagon comes and hauls you away.

(*Lewis Donohew, is a reputed communications scholar and researcher. Now down on his farm growing grapes and living close to the earth, he contemplates issues of the day from a lifetime of experience and a love of the land.*)

30.

Passing Away

Of A Dear Family Member

An entire village in Gadag, Southern State of Karnataka, India bid a tearful adieu to a cow which died while delivering a calf at a veterinary hospital in January 2011.

Cow, the pet of a farmer, was given a dignified burial.

The cow reared by farmer Balappa Buradi was helping him in agricultural works. In no time, the pet of the family - fondly called as Sita - became a darling of the neighbourhood too.

While carrying, eight-year-old Sita developed health complications and was taken to a veterinary hospital nearby. It breathed its last the next afternoon while delivering the calf.

The inconsolable family and the villagers decided to give Sita a dignified burial as a mark of respect. They draped the cow in a Ilkal saree (a local speciality) and decorated it with flowers. Married women offered poojas and stood in queue for the rituals.

Then there was beating of drums, bursting of firecrackers and singing of bhajans. The body was put on a flower-decked bullock cart for a procession in the village, and it was finally laid to rest in the farmer Buradi's farm. While mourning, the farmer said losing Sita was like losing a family member.

(From a Times of India report)

31.

Where Are The Boy Cows?

By Naomi Loewith

What happens to the boy cows?" my friend's four-year-old son asked me as we toured the farm this summer.

I exchanged a glance with his mother. Though I believe it's important for kids to understand certain things about farming, I didn't think it was my place to teach someone else's toddler where veal comes from.

"On this farm, we keep baby girl cows," I told him, "and the baby boys go to a different farm."

He looked sad, so I explained, "This farm is for milk and only girls can give milk. It's just like when you were a baby, and you drank your mom's milk."

He thought about it for a moment, then seemed satisfied and ran off to pet a day-old calf.

I'm often surprised by how many farm guests forget that cows are mammals: Only females produce milk, and they only do so after giving birth.

Bulls have a different career path. Indeed, many modern dairy farms have no bulls, as their function can be served with a monthly purchase of semen, a liquid nitrogen tank to store it and a very long glove.

> "The human race is challenged more than ever before to demonstrate our mastery - not over nature - but over ourselves."
> —Rachel Carson, Environmentalist

32.

I'm Sorry, What Was Your Name Again?

Cow Name Registry Created In Estonia

Estonia's centre for animal records has created an official registry for the names of cows in the country.

With more than half of the over 7,000 entries in the registry, "Black Cow" - "Mustik" in Estonian - was by far the most popular name. Common Estonian female names such as Ursula, Piret and Kadr were also near the top of the list.

Whats there in a name? But a person's name is the sweetest sound in the world to him or her. So it is with the cows! Yes, cows, just like us, want to be called by their names.

According to researchers at Newcastle University, calling cows by personal names makes them happy and happy cows produce more milk.

A study by the university's School of Agriculture, Food and Rural Development, involving 516 farmers across the UK, found that cows that are named and treated with a "more personal touch" can increase milk yields by up to 500 pints a year. The study, published in the journal Anthrozoos, found farmers who named their cows gained a higher yield than the 54% that did not give their cattle names. Dairy farmer Dennis Gibb, who co-owns Eachwick Red House Farm, says he believed treating every cow as an individual was "vitally important".

Farmer Dennis Gibb says "They aren't just our livelihood, they're part of the family. We love our cows here at Eachwick and every one of them has a name. Collectively we refer to them as 'our ladies' but we

know every one of them and each one has her own personality." Dr Catherine Douglas, who led the research, says: "What our study shows is what many good, caring farmers have long since believed. Our data suggests that, on the whole, dairy farmers regard their cows as intelligent beings capable of experiencing a range of emotions. Placing more importance on knowing the individual animals and calling them by name can, at no extra cost to the farmer, also significantly increase milk production."

THE AUTHOR

Dr. Sahadeva dasa (Sanjay Shah) is a monk in vaisnava tradition. Coming from a prominent family of Rajasthan, he graduated in commerce from St.Xaviers College, Kolkata and then went on to complete his CA (Chartered Accountancy) and ICWA (Cost and works Accountancy) with national ranks. Later he received his doctorate.

For close to last two decades, he is leading a monk's life and he has made serving God and humanity as his life's mission.

He has been serving as the president of ISKCON Secunderabad center since last twenty years.

His areas of work include research in Vedic and contemporary thought, Corporate and educational training, social work and counselling, travelling in India and aborad, writing books and of course, practicing spiritual life and spreading awareness about the same.

He is also an accomplished musician, composer, singer, instruments player and sound engineer. He has more than a dozen albums to his credit so far. (SoulMelodies.com) His varied interests include alternative holistic living, Vedic studies, social criticism, environment, linguistics, history, art & crafts, nature studies, web technologies etc.

His earlier books, Oil - A Global Crisis and Its Solutions (oilCrisisSolutions.com), End of Modern Civilization and Alternative future (WorldCrisisSolutions.com) have been acclaimed internationally.

OTHER BOOKS BY THE AUTHOR

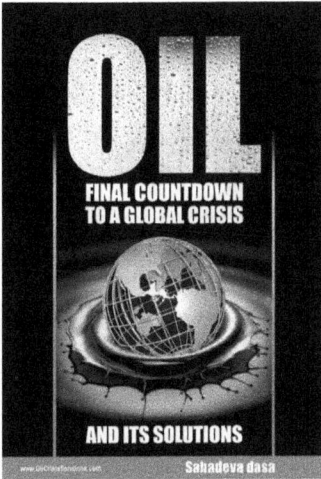

This unique book by the author examines the lifeline of modern living - petroleum. In our veins today, what flows is petroleum. Every aspect of our life, from food to transport to housing, its all petroleum based. Either its petroleum or its nothing. Our existence is draped in layers of petroleum. This book is a bible on the subject and covers every conceivable aspect of it, from its strategic importance to future prospects. Then the book goes on to delineate important strategic solutions to an unprecedented crisis thats coming our way.

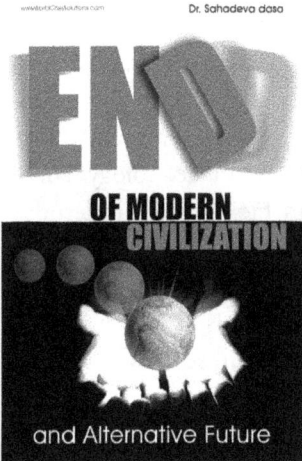

Pages-330, www.OilCrisisSolutions.com

This book by Dr Sahadeva dasa is an authoritative work in civilizational studies as it relates to our future. Dr. Dasa studied human civilizations of last 5000 years and the reasons these civilizations went into oblivion. Each of these civilizations collapsed due to presence of one or two factors like neglect of soil, moral degradation, leadership crisis etc. But in our present civilization, all the factors that brought down all the these civilizations are operational with many more additional ones. Then the book goes on to chalk out the alternative future for mankind.

Pages-440, www.WorldCrisisSolutions.com

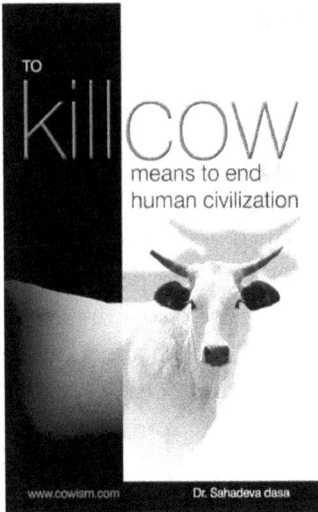

This landmark book on cow protection delineates various aspects of cow sciences as presented by the timeless voice of an old civilization, Vedas. This book goes on to prove that the cow will be the making or breaking point for humanity, however strange it may sound. Science of cow protection needs to be researched further and more attention needs to be given to this area. Most of the challenges staring in the face of mankind can be traced to our neglect in this area.

Pages-136,   www.cowism.com

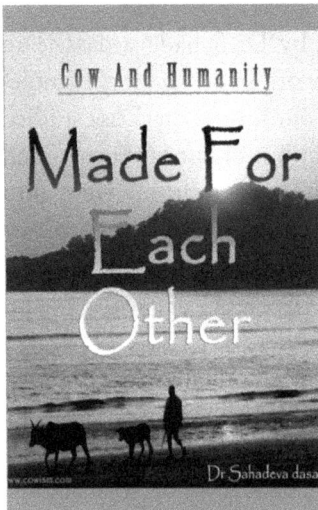

This book discusses the vital role of cows in peace and progress of human society. Among other things, it also addresses the modern ecological concerns. It emphasizes the point that 'eCOWlogy' is the original God made ecology. For all the challenges facing mankind today, mother cow stands out as the single answer.

Living with cow is living on nature's income instead of squandering her capital. In the universal scheme of creation, fate of humans has been attached to that cows, to an absolute and overwhelming degree.

Pages-144, www.cowism.com

COWS ARE COOL

Love 'Em!

DR SAHADEVA DASA

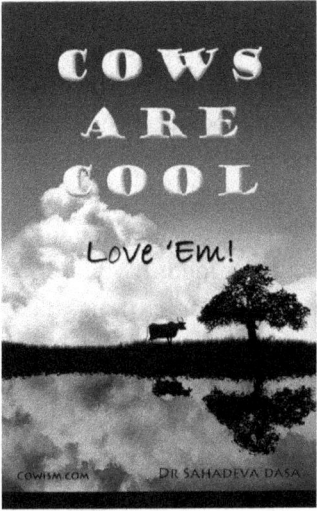

This book deals with the internal lives of the cows and contains true stories from around the world. Cow is a very sober animal and does not wag its tail as often as a dog. This does not mean dog is good and cow is food. All animals including the dog should be shown love and care. But cow especially has a serious significance for human existence in this world. Talk about cows' feelings is often brushed off as fluffy and sentimental but this book proves it otherwise.

Pages 136, www.cowism.com

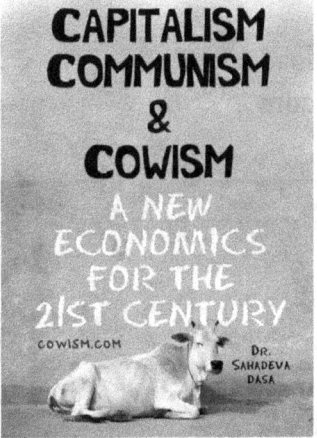

CAPITALISM COMMUNISM & COWISM

A NEW ECONOMICS FOR THE 21ST CENTURY

DR. SAHADEVA DASA

If humanity and the planet have to survive, we have to replace our present day economic model. It's a fossil fuel based, car-centred, energy inefficient model and promotes over exploitation of natural resources, encourages a throwaway society, creates social injustice and is not viable any longer.

This book presents an alternative economic system for the 21st Century. This is an economics which works for the people and the Planet.

Pages 136, www.cowism.com

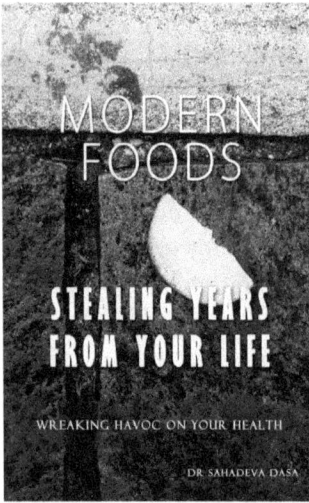

Food is our common ground, a universal experience. But there is trouble with our food. Traditional societies had good food but we just have good table manners. A disease tsunami is sweeping the world. Humanity is dying out. This is the result of our deep ignorance about our food. If you don't have good health, the other things like food, housing, transportation, education and recreation don't mean much. This books lists out major killer foods of our industrial civilization and how to escape them.

Pages 296, www.FoodcrisisSolutions.com

Music Albums: Download From
Soul Melodies.com

Music Albums: Download From
Soul Melodies.com

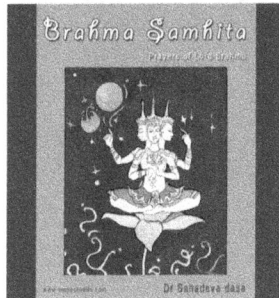

www.ingramcontent.com/pod-product-compliance
Lightning Source LLC
Chambersburg PA
CBHW050529280326
41933CB00011B/1525